CONGAN

A CELTIC SAINT OF THE ISLES

THE HIGHLANDS AND ABERDEENSHIRE

IN HISTORICAL PERSPECTIVE

by

HAROLD WALLACE GARNER

Published by TIMOLEON
1, Coastguard Station, Banff,
Aberdeenshire, Scotland, AB45 1JG UK.

The right of Mr Harold Wallace Garner to be identified as the author of this work has been asserted by him in accordance with the Copyright, Design and Patents Act 1988.

ISBN
0-9553837-0-6
978-0-9553837-0-0

Ordance Survey Maps Crown ©Copyright
and/or database. All rights reserved.
Licence number 100046323

January 2007

Printed by W. Peters & Sons Printers & Publishers
16 High Street, Turriff, AB53 4DT Tel. 01888 563589

ACKNOWLEDGEMENTS

We heartily thank the many relatives and friends who encouraged and helped us with the first and second publications of this history, especially:

The Rev. Sylvia Dyer, who suggested the research;
The Rev. Grant MacIntosh, without whose great interest and support nothing would have materialized;
Miss Anne E. Cormach and Dr Hilary Murray for their fine illustrations derived from Pictish stones;
Mr Steven Mackison of Dunlugas for the first edition of 'The Life of St Congan' in booklet form and for his help with the layout of this volume;
Mr and Mrs W Davidson of Turriff for their invaluable information about St Congan in connection with their home 'St Congan's Den';
Mr Barrie Anderson for drawing maps, proof reading, and his support;
the Hon. Michael Shaw of Seil Island for information about the island;
Mrs Hilary White, Archaeologist, the Highland Council;
Mrs N. Gatz, the Highland Council, Portree, and the Portree Historical Society;
Mr Murdo Macdonald, Archivist, Argyle and Bute Council Archives, Lochgilhead;
Mr Ian Hay, Technical Services, Highland Council Offices, Dingwall;
The Staff at the Aberdeenshire County Reference library at Old Meldrum;
The Staff at the Highland Reference Library, Inverness;
Mr Tom Dawson of the Shorewatch and Scape Trusts, North Uist;
Computing Solutions & Co, Banff, for preparing maps and timely rescues.

H W Garner
Banff 2006

INTRODUCTION

St Congan, sometimes known as Coan (pronounced 'ho-an'), Cowan, and Comgan, is patron saint of Turriff in Aberdeenshire and of Kirktown, near the Kyles of Lochalsh.

A Christian Prince of an Irish Royal House, Congan was active as a missionary in about 700 AD, give or take forty years. This volume revises 'The Life and Times of St Congan.' It was published at the suggestion of the Reverend Sylvia Dyer and the Reverend Grant MacIntosh, produced and printed for me by Mr Steven Mackison, the proceeds to be given to the Rose Window Fund of the Episcopal Church Turriff, which is dedicated to St Congan.

The edition was too limited. It sold out. A reprint was needed. I started correcting and revising. The expanded second edition you are about to read, not only is an account of St Congan's life, but also mentions related traditions and ancient commercial activities in Scotland that have had their part in the history of the Highlands and North East of Scotland.

Pictish Scotland may be better understood if the interconnecting histories of contemporary peoples on the Mediterranean and Atlantic Coast are mentioned; and how, in the remote past, the Phœnicians, the Carthaginians, and the Greeks of Massilia (Marseilles), plied an Atlantic trade route from the Mediterranean to the isles of the Inner Hebrides, the Scottish mainland, and the Moray Firth; and how St Congan came to place thirteen of his chapels or churches where he did.

Piecing together the remote past is, at best, informed guesswork. The test of this account is whether it makes enough sense to be accepted as a working hypothesis upon which others may establish some or all of its interpretations as more than probabilities.

H W Garner
Banff 2006

CHAPTERS

Page

1   1. The Atlantic Coast Trade - the Phœnicians.

5   2. The Atlantic Coast Trade - the Carthaginians.

8   3. The Greeks of Massilia, the Romans, and the sudden end of the Atlantic Coast Trade.

11   4. The Mediterranean Traders in Britain.

18   5. The Iron Age on the Moray Firth.

21   6. Four Ancient Trackways.

27   7. The Churches and Chapels of St Congan.

46   8. Balmellie Crofts, Turriff.

49   9. Cowan's or Congan's Den, Turriff.

51   10. St Congan - His Life and Times.

60   11. A Social Scourge of Ancient Times.

63   12. The River Deveron and the town of Banff.

68   13. St Congan's Den - The Modern Dwelling.

CHAPTER 1
THE ATLANTIC COAST TRADE - THE PHŒNICIANS

Recent historical research into the Bronze, Copper, and Iron Ages has added much knowledge about trade along the European Atlantic Coast between the peoples of the Mediterranean and the British Isles in those times.

This trade extended, over time, to include the Pictish Celts in the Highlands and those of them that had migrated eastwards and then inland from the shores of the Moray Firth. In their time, Picts living on the Moray Firth coast traded with Carthaginians and Greeks from the Mediterranean, bartering ambergris they found on its shores, and amber, which the Jutes, forerunners of the Danish voyagers, brought across the North Sea from the shores of the Baltic Sea.

The Tartessians, a Celtic tribe living on the Atlantic coast were the first to trade with Britain. The Phœnicians were next to sail the same Atlantic route, first arriving in Britain in about 700 BC, sailing every summer afterwards on trading expeditions to the Scilly Isles which they called the Tin Islands. When they ceased coming, the Carthaginians continued the trade; that is until the destruction of their city of Carthage by the Romans. After that event the Greeks of the city of Massilia, now known as Marseilles, took over the trade.

They were experienced ocean mariners. In very early times, before even the days of the legendary Queen of Sheba who lived in neighbouring Yemen, they lived on the shores of the Arabian Sea in what is now the Oman. From there they sailed the monsoon winds to the west coast of India for trade with the Goans. Long before Homer told of the Trojan War, some of these skilled sailors migrated to the Mediterranean, to a land with a plentiful supply of large cedar trees and oaks suitable for ship-building. Here they founded several cities, including Tyre. Their land was known as Phœnicia, after that Canaan, and now as the Lebanon.

They revolutionized sailing in the Mediterranean. In their large ships, the 'ships of Tarshish' mentioned in Kings, Isaiah, and Ezekiel, of the Christian Holy Bible, instead of hugging the coast, day-sailing as was Mediterranean practice, they sailed out of sight of land for days at a time directly to Sicily or Malta, and on to Spain. They were able to make these voyages because, at night, they sailed courses plotted from stars they had arranged into constellations which we know by the names they gave them. These early voyages were, to a large extent, state expeditions. The Phoenicians and the colonists they had planted in Carthage, now Tunis, were not chancy adventurers. They, and the Greeks of Massilia, were civilized and very well educated. Their cities had written constitutions. Zeno, the philosopher, who proposed the 'Hare and Tortoise' mathematical riddle, was a Phœnician living in Athens. Tacitus (56 -117AD) says of the Greeks of Massilia that they were rather severe in their manner, and that "elegant gravity always distinguished their city".

The Phœnicians were the first to venture out of the Mediterranean and make deep-sea voyages into the Atlantic. During the day they used a sun-compass, knowledge of which was lost to the western world after the time of the Vikings; that is until one was discovered recently in a Viking ship-burial at Greenland. The sun compass is a portable sun-dial. It consists of a pillar mounted upon a small rectangular board, the tip of which casts a shadow on an arc marked on the board. By orientating the board so the tip of the shadow touches the arc as the sun changes altitude during the day, true north is indicated at that moment for that latitude. Thick cloud makes the device useless. For such occasions when far out to sea, the Viking explorers had a word in their language meaning "despair at being lost in a watery desolation not knowing which way to sail".

When the Phœnicians made their Atlantic voyages to the north they sailed along the Iberian coast for a short distance until they reached a particular island, a rather small one, close inshore to the city of Tartessa. They favoured this kind of island as a suitable trading post. The tiny island of St Michael's Mount in Cornwall is typical.

The Tartessians were Celts. Their city was on the site of Cadiz. Long before the Phœnicians arrived, this tribe had been sailing annually to the Scilly Isles, off the coast of Cornwall, for tin mined there by the Cornish Celts. This tin, and their local-mined silver, they traded with whomsoever came to Tartessa.

They adventured. The Tartessians, and the Phœnicians in their time, are believed to have crossed the Atlantic Ocean, because Tartessian inscriptions have been found at Mount Hope Bay, Rhode Island, North America, and, it is claimed, a Phœnician inscription has been found in Brazil.

It was customary for Mediterranean peoples to set up twin pillars at the beginning of every major trading route leading to distant lands. Accordingly, in a prominent position on this small island next to Tartessa, the Phœnicians set up twin stone pillars which some say were quite modest, about three metres high, which they dedicated to Hercules. They then let it be known that these, the Pillars of Hercules, the name by which the island was afterwards known, marked the border of their Atlantic trading area; and that from henceforth the Atlantic Ocean was their private property and others would be prevented from entering it; excepting, of course, those from Carthage, their daughter colony.

'The Pillars of Hercules' now became an important entrepôt. Some two hundred years later, the inevitable happened. Soon after 500 BC, the Phœnicians waged war upon the Tartessians, whom they defeated. They then occupied their city, renaming it Gades (Phœnician = 'fortress'), rebuilding its great temple that had long been dedicated by the Tartessians to Hercules/Melkart. Later, in the time of the Carthaginians, the priests at this temple were celibate. They had their heads and faces shaved, and wore distinctive robes; imitated much later to some extent by Christian monks in Europe.

After the consequent loss of Tartessian ships, Phœnician trade goods were transferred into those built and manned by another tribe, the Venetii, who lived further north, in Brittany, on the shores of the Morbihan (Breton-Celtic 'mor' = sea + 'bihan' = little).

It should be mentioned that, by now, the Phœnicians were in force at the western end of the Mediterranean. They had colonies at the sites of present day Torre del Mar and San Christóbal near Almünécar, places not unknown to holidaymakers from Scotland. The great natural wealth of Spain was solely at their disposal. In his book, 'The Greeks of the West', A. G. Woodhead says that at this time precious metals, predominantly silver, were found on and near the surface, that the Iberian Celts could mine 57 lbs, avoirdupois, of silver in three days. He says the Phœnicians at Gades issued silver coinage, and those from Tyre would hammer the lead off their anchors and replace it with silver for the homeward voyage.

Sailing to Britain for tin now took on another dimension. Previously, the Tartessians and the Venetii had kept to inshore routes, day-sailing to their destinations on the Atlantic seaboard. When voyaging with the Phœnicians they combined their nautical knowledge.

Julius Caesar, the chief source of information, noted in his account 'Gallic Wars' that in his time the Venetii ships were between twelve and fifteen metres long, of between 500 to 600 tonnes burden, that they had leathern sails that would withstand wear and tear from the Atlantic winds; and that they were sturdier and more suitable than Mediterranean ships for sailing on the north Atlantic Ocean. Cæsar also wrote that, "the Veneti, long since a seagoing tribe, had the largest fleet of ships in the north Atlantic Ocean. In these they trafficked with Britain, compelling nearly all others that sailed the Atlantic to pay toll." Other than those of ancient Athens, the oldest regulations in the western world, governing the chartering of ships, are the Laws of Oleron, an island off Brest, significantly not far from the Morbihan, where they were promulgated. No doubt, over centuries of trade, some Phœnicians and the Carthaginians did sail in their own ships to Britain. Indeed, Strabo the historian, who was governor of this part of Spain in about 96 BC, says the Gades ship-builders constructed more and better merchant ships for use in the Mediterranean and Atlantic waters than any other people. From that statement it is easy to assume these ships were for the British trade. Much more likely is that they were modelled upon Tartessian ships that traded along the west coast of Africa; a trade known to have extended to the island of Mogador six hundred miles to the south of Gades. It may have been that the existence of the Canaries and Madeira was a secret of the Tartessians passed on by them to the Carthaginians. Nonetheless, at the time of Alexander's return to the Middle East, the Mediterranean ports were full of rumours that ships from Gades had succeeded in sailing round the continent of Africa from west to east, (there were previous attempts, all unsuccessful). These rumours would have reached the ears of Alexander the Great and encouraged him in his plans to march round its perimeter, which, came to nothing because he died before he could implement them.

Many customs and ideas of these times survived through the ages. The Phœnicians and the Carthaginians worshipped Hercules; but only as a demi-god, because he was fathered by Zeus upon an earthly woman. Curiously, centuries later, the founding fathers of Christianity after much discussion improved upon this kind of belief, they deciding that, though Christ was similarly fathered, he is fully a divine element of a 'three-in-one' deity. This decision parallels Celtic and Indian belief that some gods and goddesses have triple aspects. Many Druids, when it came to their conversion, well understood the nature of the equality between the holy components of the 'Trinity', as written into the Nicene Creed and recited at the services of most Christian Churches through the ages to this day.

The Phœnicians, their trade and influence, disappeared abruptly from the Mediterranean, and from the Atlantic, in about 340 BC. This happened after Alexander of Macedonia attacked their cities of Sidon and Tyre, especially Tyre, when securing his rear before marching eastwards to conquer the world. After a long siege, he destroyed Tyre with great savagery, sweeping on to Egypt, which he would have conquered had it not surrendered. Of the survivors from Tyre, men were slain and women and children sold to the slavers that followed the camp for this purpose. Their depopulated coastal land was occupied soon afterwards by the Israelites.

No more was heard of the Phœnicians as a people from Tyre.

CHAPTER 2
THE ATLANTIC COAST TRADE - THE CARTHAGINIANS

The Carthaginians continued the early Atlantic coast trade with Britain as their exclusive perquisite until about 329 BC. This was the year that Alexander of Macedonia, now called Alexander the Great, having returned from India and was at Suza in what is now southwest Iran. Here, he declared that for his next venture he would conquer Africa by marching round its coast until he arrived at his starting point from the opposite direction.

This utterance from the conqueror of the Medes and Persians and many other nations, spread like wildfire around the Mediterranean. It caused alarm among the Carthaginians, because whichever way round Africa he went, Carthage was on his line of march. They had no intention of surrendering but they remembered his brutal destruction of their parent city Tyre, which had resisted him.

They made contingency plans. They decided that when Alexander marched in their direction, they would abandon their city and withdraw to the Canary Isles; at that time completely unknown to other peoples of the Mediterranean There is that story, come down to us through the ages, about 'falling over the edge of the world if one went too far out to sea'. This was invented and put about by the Carthaginians as part of keeping the Canary Isles, Madeira, and the Azores a secret to themselves; even though generations of educated people knew the world was a rotating sphere, and everyone in the Mediterranean knew Carthaginian traders as professional liars.

In implementing these plans, the Carthaginians let the Greeks of Massilia join them in the Atlantic with the object of their taking over the trade whilst they, the Carthaginians, restricted themselves to trading with Spain and the west coast of Africa from the Canaries.

That is how the Massiliote Greeks became involved with an hitherto exclusive sea trade to Britain.

However, after making his plans to conquer Africa known, Alexander died at Babylon in the following year. The Carthaginians, though relieved of the fear of their destruction, did not cancel the permission they had given the Greeks of Massillia to enter the Atlantic, and both peoples made annual voyages to the Tin Isles for another 184 years, the Massiliotes for longer.

Rome was a rising power. She had been at war with Carthage since 264 BC.

The Romans called them the Punic Wars, deriving the name rom the Latin 'Pœnicus' = Phœnician, the Romans regarding both as the same people.

The Punic Wars were in fact, three great conflicts. The last, in 146 BC, ended in the destruction of Carthage by the Roman general Scipio Æmillianus.

In one respect, however, there was a marked psychological difference between the Carthaginians and other peoples of the Mediterranean.

The Carthaginians had an extraordinarily dark side to their minds.

They were obsessed with thoughts of evil forces in a way that was devastating to themselves. They believed they were surrounded by hordes of evil powers against whom they waged war ceaselessly in unequal combat.

Scipio Æmillianus, statesman and conquering general, highly regarded in his time and long afterwards as a man of high culture and learning, remarked upon this obsession. When viewing the prows or 'beaks' taken from Carthaginian fighting ships captured after the final sea battle of the last Punic war, he is recorded as saying of the figureheads, all of contorted demons, "Carthage never lacked for nightmares, and when we killed her she passed them on to us."

Scipio Æmillianus may have had more insight than he knew. Deducing from the daily presentations on TV and film of ghastly evil and grisly horror, imagined by so many of our present-day writers and producers of fiction, then disseminated to millions of people; it would seem those Carthaginian nightmares not only crossed the Mediterranean to Rome, but came along the Atlantic Trade Route to us. These same nightmares would seem to be with us today, distorting our minds similarly: to give but one instance – the way in which we collectively sacrifice to the goddess of speed and accept the carnage on our roads.

The nightmarish qualities of the Carthaginians' continuous battle against devilish powers led to their taking desperate actions based upon harsh logic.

For strength, the Carthaginians had conflated Hercules with their less powerful god, Melkarth, to whom they had long since offered sacrifices in return for favours. As the case with all semetic gods, the greater the favour asked, the greater the sacrifice required; more so, when the favours for which the Cathaginians were asking required the sacrifice of children; to the disgust of the Greeks, Romans, and most other Mediterranean people.

During the desperate final stages of the last Punic war, great numbers of children were sacrificed. Most Carthaginians now found they were sacrificing their own children, those of slaves having already gone to the altar; praying at the same time to Melkarth's consort, a goddess named Tanit, asking her to give their dead children her personal special care and love in their after-life.

Evidence of these tragedies was revealed by archæologists excavating among the ruins of Carthage in the 1970's. They discovered the remains of hundreds of children in burial grounds created especially for them.

In passing, it should be said that Tanit, the carer of these murdered children, was depicted as having one of her hands coloured red. The Carthaginians trading along the Atlantic Coast brought a cult of 'the Red Hand of Tanit' to the peoples there, and this passed down through the generations in talismanic variations which exist to this day, as mentioned in Chapter 4.

CHAPTER 3

THE GREEKS OF MASSILIA, THE ROMANS, & THE SUDDEN END OF THE ATLANTIC COAST TRADE

The last-comers to the trade with Britain were Greeks from Massilia, now known as Marseilles, a city founded on the Mediterranean coast of France east of the estuary of the River Rhone in 600 BC by Greeks from Ionic Phocæa. The Phocæan Greeks founded five other colonies in Spain at about the same time, to act as bases for trade with the Celts in Gaul and Spain, of whom the Massiliotes taught many to read and write, giving an academic education to important men.

The earliest substantiated written record of a circumnavigation of Britain is of one, perhaps more, made between the years 332-330 BC by Pitheas, a Greek from Massilia. His voyages, which his fellow citizens funded, were for exploration and scientific purposes. He sailed round Britain seeking the places of origin of tin, ambergris, amber, and gold, all of which the Carthaginians were bringing back to the Mediterranean, as did the Phœnicians and Tartessians before them.

He reported he found no amber on the coast of Britain. However, on one of his voyages, he found it on the shores of the Baltic Sea where it originates.

There were three Amber Routes from Jutland, one to the east and two to the Mediterranean. The western one of these two first crossed the North Sea and passed along the coast of the Moray Firth to the Cromarty Firth. From there it led overland, through Strath Bran and Glen Carron, to the beach at Kirkton, Lochalsh, from whence it was shipped south on the Atlantic Coast Trade Route.

Pytheas was already known as a skilled astronomer and observer. He had noted that the tides were synchronized with the moon's motion. He took latitudes from star sights, especially the Pole Star, in relation to landmarks and places visited on his voyages. Later, his observations came into the hands of the astronomer Hipparchus (c.150 BC), who used them when making his map of northern and central Europe. Latitudes were essential both for map-making and the making of sun compasses which only worked for the latitude in which they were to be used. There were no magnetic compasses.

Pytheas's information enabled the geographer Eratosthenes (c 235 BC) to locate Ireland's position relative to Britain, and to name and mark the relative positions of the big rivers of the Atlantic seaboard. As reported by Pliny, perhaps the most authentic information Pytheas reported is that he observed from a shore in the north, seas of 30 metres high when the wind was against the tide. The only place in the British Isles where this can happen is in the Pentland Firth during a strong gale. This could only mean he had been overlooking the sea from one of its shores. He was the first to provide information that put the Moray Firth on the map.

In those times geographic positions were difficult to ascertain. Bearings and latitudes were taken with reference to the winter or summer rising and setting of the sun. A set of standardized adjustments was used for each week between March and September, and another for the rest of the year. Bearings taken ashore during the day were cross-checked the same night with the observed latitude of the Pole Star in the constellation of the 'Great Bear'. This system worked well enough on the coasts of the Mediterranean Sea where latitudes vary only slightly. In the north of Scotland at times the sun's position on the horizon noticeably varies between each successive sunset, or sunrise. Sometimes the difference between the sun's position on the horizon, and its position twenty-four hours later, is quite considerable. When used in the north, the means of calculation were not adequate to the task, which brought about some interesting map-making.

Four hundred and forty years or so later, when the map-maker Ptolemy (85 - 165 AD) came to draw a map of England and Scotland from Pytheas's data, he set the whole of Scotland at almost a right angle to the rest of Britain, north pointing to east or nearly so. This happened because the latitudes supplied by Pytheas, made in relation to the summer sunset-sunrise bearings, had been adjusted twice in the wrong direction; Pytheas not being able to see the Pole Star to confirm his observations. Stars are not visible in northern Scotland during the continuous twilights of June.

The next important event affecting the Atlantic trade occurred immediately after 146 BC, the last year of the three Punic wars. Athens and Carthage were much older than Rome. Athens became part of the Roman Empire, and Rome bided her time. Only when she became as powerful as Carthage did the intolerable situation arise in the Mediterranean that resulted in the Punic Wars. In the last year of third war the Romans destroyed the city of Carthage, and its people, so utterly that they disappeared from history.

The Greeks of Massilia, on the south coast of Gaul, now France, had been allies of the Carthaginians. The Romans, appreciating that the Massilians, had been forced to choose and had chosen the side that lost, dealt with them unusually leniently, exacted a large fine, but allowed them to continue trading with the Tin Isles.

Nearly a century later, in 50 BC, Cæsar conquered Gaul. Earlier he had deliberately destroyed the Venetii-Gauls in a sea battle off Brest in the same period. The Venetii never had need of fighting ships, never having been attacked by another fleet. Cæsar built a fleet and sought the battle especially to destroy them. His intention was to divert the lucrative Atlantic Coast trade through Gaul, now under Roman rule, and thus place it entirely into Roman hands.

He was successful. After the battle, the trade from Britain to the Mediterranean went through the channel ports of Dover, Calais, Southampton, and Boulogne.

A year later, in 49 BC, Julius Cæsar besieged Massilia. The city surrendered and, as the author, A. Trevor Hodge, says in his book 'Ancient Greek France', "It became Rome's window on Gaul; an ideal centre for gathering intelligence, more or less in the way Berlin was in the days of the Cold War." Mention might be made here of a report from the time that says, "the wine from Massillia is always excellent".

Transport of tin, overland, was expensive. Later, when the Emperor Augustus opened the tin mines in Spain, the Romans abandoned the Cornish mines. By this time the Greeks of Massliia, the Massiliotes, no longer traded directly with the Celts of Britain. Instead, as staunch allies of Julius Cæsar, they developed existing trade with the Gauls by way of the River Rhone.

The ships of the Venetii no longer existed. The Atlantic Coast Trade ceased. Drugs, pottery, and iron ingots that reached the settlements in the hinterland of the Moray Firth now came from the south. Whether ambergris and amber were traded in return is not known.

CHAPTER 4
THE MEDITERRANEAN TRADERS IN BRITAIN

As they traded along the Atlantic coast, the Carthaginians spread their way of life, names, and symbols associated with it, especially the 'Red Hand of Tanit'. A red hand, appears in Breton and in Cornish folklore. Further north, in Wales is the heraldic 'Bloody Hand of Chark, and across the Irish Sea, the present-day 'Red Hand of Ulster'. In Scotland, the mother of St Kentigern, (known also as St Mungo, patron saint of Glasgow), herself a convert to Christianity, was called St Thenew, a corruption of Tanit.

It is well known that trade with foreigners not only brings goods but also especially new and strange religious notions. It was the murderous trait in the Carthaginian psyche that prompted their traders, with the best of intentions, to introduce the idea of human sacrifice to the Celts of southern Britain; thus ending in Britain a benign way of life managed by the Druids that had lasted for thousands of years.

Archæological evidence of the presence of the Mediterranean people in Britain is rare but it exists. The remains of a very ancient wreck of a timbered ship at the entrance to the river Erme, Bigbury Bay, on the south Devon, carbon-dated to very early times, had the remains of ingots of very pure tin and with them a small female figurine, possibly of the Carthaginian goddess, Tanit. This is an unusual find because a Carthaginian ship usually carried a seated figurine of the dwarf god, Baal, as its guardian deity. The wreck may have been that of a Venetii ship on charter to the Carthaginians and the figurine from a later time when Tanit was the supreme deity.

A similar Baal figurine was dug up near the site of an old tin smelting house, a copy of which is in the Cornwall County Museum at Truro. From this and other evidence, it seems that the Cornish miners adopted Baal from the Carthaginians as protector and working-wizard for the tin smelting process, and that they revered him as such until very recent times. Some think the Carthaginian influence reached the far north and that the seated king in the chess set found in 1831 at Uig on the Isle of Lewis, has a resemblance to the same figure of Baal because three marks on that figurine's chest are also found on the chess pieces.

Baal was considered a protecting god, not only by the tin-miners of Cornwall but also by the Picts. Baal found his way into Celtic language as 'buachaille' (pronounced bucca'), one of its earliest meanings is an isolated rock standing, shepherd-like, on an hillside, which later came to mean any prominent isolated hill. The Bin of Cullen on the Moray coast had 'buachaille' as an earlier name. With its lower companions the Little Bin and the Hill of Maud, from a distance at sea it is an excellent landmark for the port of Buckie, a variant of 'bucca', being derived from the landmark's earlier name.

Eventually 'bucca' came to mean a shepherd or cowherd, and then a comrade. As such it was once a common term of familiarity amongst the Scots, especially of Glasgow. As late as the beginning of the last century, Neil Munro (1863-1930), the author of 'Para Handy', uses it at least once in his stories of a fictional Mr Jimmy Swan the travelling salesman of whom he writes as saluting a young friend as 'my bucca'. The term fell into disuse after the Oscar Wilde trial and conviction in 1895.

There is social evidence of the presence of Phœnicians and Carthaginians in Britain. Culinary dishes of visitors to these shores are readily assimilated, as is well known. The Phœnicians are said to have brought to Britain the crocus bulb that provides saffron, still thriving in Cornwall where it is grown to this day. The Cornish use it for colouring their cooking. The Carthaginians are said to have brought a rare breed of fallow deer (dama dama), indigenous to north Africa, to Mount Edgcumbe, an estate bordering the sea at Plymouth Sound, where their descendants still live.

The legend, saying a Phœnician taught the Cornish how to purge tin of its wolfram, and the belief that Baal's intervention was needed in this process, has been mentioned. When the early missionaries came to Britain they adapted this legend, substituting St Joseph of Aramathea for the unknown Phœnician metal-smith, claiming it was not Baal, but rather, the infant Jesus he bought to Britain with him. This legend about a Phœnician has a ring of truth about it, because, as not a few have remarked, semitic peoples are not unlike each other to the northern eye. Nonetheless, William Blake embraced fully a legend, that appears to have been Christianized, in his poem which he entitled 'And did those feet in ancient times walk upon England's Mountains Green', otherwise known as "Jerusalem."

Geoffrey of Monmouth, he who adapted the stories of King Arthur to please his monarch, in writing about another pre-Christian legend says that a Carthaginian man named Brutus, grandson of Aeneas, the Trojan hero who fathered a son on Dido, Queen of Carthage, landed at Totnes, Devon. More likely the man who landed at Totnes, a most ancient port, was a Carthaginian trader who, for the purpose of inflating his importance, a common practice throughout the ages amongst the profiteering fraternity, had said, to impress, that he was a son of Æneas and Dido.

Samuel Bochart in his book 'Geographia Sacra' (1649) suggests the name Britannia is a variant of the Phœnician word 'Bartanac' which means 'land of tin'; making his point by saying the Britons were not unified enough to call either themselves British or their land Britain.

A man named Bawden noted his opinion in the 'Western Antiquary' (December 1882), published in Devon and Cornwall, that all British surnames ending in 'is' such as Harris, Davis, Lewis, Ellis, Morris, etc., are of Phœnician origin. A search of Landnámabók, a 13th Century record of some two hundred names that are mentioned in the Norse sagas, reveals no name ending in 'is' though Harris and Lewis are names of two isles of the Hebrides, once part of a Viking kingdom. It would seem these may well be Phœnician and not Viking names, so Samuel Bochart may be correct in this respect. It should be said that the suffix 'son' attached to many, if not all of these names, is a later accretion in keeping with Viking practice.

The 13th century Welsh Book of Taliesin, has material culled from Celtic sources in Britain that date back before the times of the Romans. It includes a poem containing the vestiges of a Bardic song that mentions Hercules. Reports say that, towards the end of the Carthaginian influence on the Celts living on the Atlantic Coast of southern Britain, giant wickermen, token resemblances of Melkarth/Hercules, were erected in places. It is said, people were caged alive within these, as offerings, and the wickermen set alight: a variant of Carthaginian sacrificial practices to their god, reflecting contemporary happenings in Carthage, and indicating the presence of Carthaginian traders and their religious horrors. This practice spread from Britain to Gaul, but, after the destruction of Carthage, it ceased in both places as soon as the Romans established control. It should be said that, where the Druids were respected, the British Celts did not kill defeated opponents.

As for evidence of the presence of the Greeks of Massilia in Britain, one needs seek no further than the ancient annual May Day celebrations, suppressed in 1837 and revived in 1974, at the little fishing port of Padstow on the north coast of Cornwall, a vital safe harbour of passage and staging-port for the Mediterranean traders. In ancient days it had a wide and deep natural lagoon, made useless to shipping in the 18th and 19th centuries by vast quantities of sand carried down from tin mines.

Here, on the first minute after midnight, one of two grotesque figures, known now as either as 'the red ribbon hobby hoss' and 'the blue ribbon hobby hoss', appears in the streets to the strains of a haunting tune sung by its entourage of townsfolk.

Each masked figure is a man wearing a pointed hat and a shoulder-high circular frame two metres or so in diameter from which a skirt is suspended round its perimeter so that it reaches the ground, much like that which a hobby-horse rider would wear. The mask has a short square-cut, Assyrian-type, beard.

Both 'hosses' never appear in the streets together because the one symbolizes winter and the lifeless world of Hades, the other, the spring and summer of Demeter and virility. The costumes have changed a little, though plastic materials have done much to cheapen the ceremony which has now become a tourist attraction. The 'blue ribbon hoss', in time past, was once known as the 'black hoss'. When a certain verse is sung, now gibberish after many years of being passed from mouth to mouth, the 'hoss' pretends to die, only to spring into life at the singing of the next verse. The chorus of the song, 'Unite, and Unite', bids all hearers to do what is needed to ensure another generation; an injunction that would have been inappropriate at the celebrations of the Mysteries in Athens those thousands of years ago.

This song, sung by the followers of each 'hoss', welcomes Spring to Padstow. Its style and purpose suggest that something like it was sung thousands of years ago during the celebrations of the Mysteries of Demeter and Persephoné. These Mysteries took place annually at Athens, and later were copied at other Greek and Roman cities. They mark the occasion when Persephoné temporarily left her husband, dark Hades, to rejoin her mother, Demeter, who then, and only then, let flowers bloom and crops grow.

This benign cult spread over all the Greek and Roman worlds with sites in many places. It lasted two thousand years, fading into insignificance through old age at the time of the coming of Christianity, but not because of it. Men, women, children, and slaves, could and did become initiates, as did many Roman emperors and philosophers. The Massiliotes would certainly have brought a truncated version of the Mysteries to Britain, as a matter of course. The haunting cadences of the song, when sung well, do imply this was the case.

At Padstow, this great Greek Mystery appears to have merged with one from Carthage because when one of these grotesque 'hoss' figures appears mysteriously from within the town, as if from nowhere, as did Persephoné from the dark bowels of the earth in the glorious part of the Mysteries: instead of bringing joy as she did, they menace the onlookers as demons.

It would seem the mystery of Demeter and Persephoné is now become a travesty enacted every May Day; equalled by that other travesty of the solemn rites of Celtic New Year, Halloween, with its grotesque masks and pointed hats. It would seem that great mysteries and religions are fated to end as banalities.

The suggestion that the Carthaginians were at Padstow is reinforced by the fact that each 'hoss' dancer wears a tall, black, pointed hat, similar to that worn by a Welsh woman in traditional dress, as John Twynne (c.1560), master of the free grammar school at Canterbury, noted. In his 'De Rebus Albionicus Britannicus', he argued that the garb of Welsh women of his time (today's Welsh traditional costume) was a survival of a Phœnician form of dress. He says also that the word 'caer', meaning fort, a term much used in the South West of Britain and Wales, was also Phœnician. In his support, it should be remembered that Wales, also on the Early Atlantic Coast Trade Route, is only some 90 nautical miles to the north of Padstow; with a fair wind, a long summer's day sail for a trader.

Trading voyages to Britain were annual happenings.

Early in the month of May, as soon as the winter constellation of the Gemini, protectors of sailors, ceases to rise, a fleet sails for the Tin Isles, as Britain was known. It sailed from the Pillars of Hercules, the island very near Tartessus, a city later known as Gades. To set sail when one's deities are not in the sky watching, may seem strange. The logic is that summer seas are not dangerous so the protection of the twin gods is not needed.

The fleet made landfall at the Scilly Isles. The outward and return voyages each lasted between ten to eighteen days.

As has been said, the Venetii were coastal pilots of great experience. Strabo (64 BC - AD 24), in his 'Geography', quotes information taken from sailing instructions about the Spanish Atlantic coast, which he had from the Venetii, mentioning lighthouses and beacons. The Phœnicians and Carthaginians, navigating by the stars, could voyage out of sight of land as they first did when they came to the Mediterranean. They used the constellation of the Little Bear to find the Pole Star. The Greeks soon learned from the Phœnicians. They catalogued the stars into the constellations we know. Later, they used the 'pointers' stars in the Great Bear to find the Pole Star. A summer voyage on the

Atlantic presented no difficulty to a ship's company of the Punic people and the Venetii, their skills being complementary.

From the Scilly Isles some ships sailed the south Cornish shore; others the north Cornish and Devon coast, crossing St George's Channel for the Gower peninsula on the south Welsh coast.

The Carthaginians, however, rarely traded up the English Channel further than the south coast of Devon for several reasons. It may be that their ship-masters, the Venetii, found the further east one sails the narrower the Channel becomes; tides and tidal currents became increasingly stronger and more dangerous, and navigation becomes more and more difficult. Further, the prevailing south-westerly winds might well delay departures from further east until the following year, causing unprofitable delay. On the other hand, crossing the English Channel between the shores of north Brittany and those of Cornwall and Devon, is not as hazardous because the tidal streams are more or less at right angles to the course made good.

The Celts in Britain expected these traders to arrive every year. In some places they had adopted a Mediterranean custom, ancient at the time, of launching a model boat to invoke the coming of the summer trading fleet.

This custom survives to this day at Cawsand, a place on the Cornish side of Plymouth Sound. Here, every year on the first day of May, as was done in ancient times at the beginning of the sailing season in the Mediterranean, a model sailing boat is ceremonially launched, preferably on an outgoing evening tide. It is a lack-lustre ceremony; as with the ceremony at Padstow, the original reason for its existence having long since been forgotten.

The first traders did not arrive in Britain until nearly the end of May. They brought wine, olive oil, medical drugs, salt, and pottery, which they exchanged for a guaranteed cargo of tin ore, to be stored locally ready for collection on the return voyage after visiting Ireland for copper and gold, and Scotland for amber and ambergris.

In the earlier period of trading, few slaves, if any, were taken. The Druids would have prevented that from happening. It is doubtful if many slaves were taken in later days because they would be a trouble and expense to transport by sea and have little saleable value, their not knowing any language other than their own, or having any sophisticated skills. It was cheaper to kidnap people from along the coasts of the Mediterranean; a sea permanently infested with pirates who kept the slave-markets, commonplace in every major town, supplied through middlemen.

The last stage of the return voyages to Gades was from the mainland of Cornwall or the Scilly Isles. It would take place preferably between the beginning of August and the first day of September, that is, before the first of the equinoctial gales.

By the time of the later Iron Age in Britain, the Carthaginians, in Venetii ships, were going to the Isle of Man in the middle of the Irish Sea en route to Iona. Tides and the safest navigation made Iona a natural way-station and base for trading among the Islands and along the West Coast of Scotland. A voyage from the Scilly Isles to Iona and back would require, at the least, twenty-eight days in reasonable weather. In one sailing season, this allowed the traders to spend June and the beginning of July in the far north.

One of the commercial reasons for the voyage was to trade iron ingots obtained locally for amber and ambergris, and for wolf and bear furs. The Mediterranean traders, before they left Cornwall or Wales to go north, would lodge such return cargoes of tin and gold as they had, in one of the many promontory forts they themselves had built for the purpose on the coast of Cornwall and Wales. They left their goods under the care of a local chief. There was never a question of theft. If the chief were dishonest, he and his tribe would not see another trader for a very long time. Then the traders would sail to their ancient stronghold on the Gower peninsula, South Wales. There they would load iron ingots brought by British tribesmen from the mines of the Forest of Dean, which is on the Welsh side of the Severn estuary. These iron ingots were bartered with the Picts. Returning from the Highlands in ballast, some ships would call at the mines at the Great Orme, Llandudno, North Wales, to pick up a cargo of high grade copper ore.

Some ships went to Iona and on from there to Lochalsh, the western end of the overland route to the coasts of the Moray Firth. This, it would seem, was as far north as they sailed. It was Pytheas, the Massiliote, mentioned earlier, who went to the Orkneys and sailed on to the edges of the polar icefield, describing ice as 'floating concrete'.

Much is written of the spread of metal tools in the Copper, the Bronze, and the Iron Ages, but rarely mentioned is how the knowledge to work these metals was acquired, possibly because it was thought to be self-evident. However, it should be said that with the metal ore and tools for working the metal came the metal-smiths, those men of magic skilled in turning rock into metal. It was these metal-smiths, travelling one, perhaps two, at a time, who brought the arcane knowledge of smelting and forging to Britain. It seems that eventually they came to the Highlands with their ingots, committed to stay until the next sailing season. These are matters for the next chapter.

CHAPTER 5
THE IRON AGE ON THE MORAY FIRTH COAST

Let us suppose an iron-smith, intent upon trading his iron ingots and his skills along the Morayshire coast, is leaving a Venetii ship at Lochalsh. The beach he lands upon is where it is today, although now far above high water. Boats and people would be there from the outer islands, from Ireland, Wales and Cornwall, and further. In his time, and centuries later in St Congan's time, this was a much-used summer landing place. When the latter saw so many people passing through, he built a missionary church on the spot. He chose well. Immediately above the present beach stands the present Scottish Episcopalian church dedicated to him.

Our iron-smith would first make his way to the settlements at Glen Carron and then pass through Strath Bran. Iron tools were expensive. The local market was limited. Once this was satisfied, he would go further afield. To do this he would embark in a local boat and sail from the Cromarty Firth to the shores of the Moray Firth, to landing-places that had trackways leading inland to settlements.

At the places where charcoal was available, he would set up his furnace. In passing it should be mentioned that, in Devon and Cornwall, archaeologists have been finding tiny sites thought to have been used for this purpose. Here, he would exchange his newly-made iron, and iron tools, for ambergris; a waxy aromatic substance related to cholesterol that is formed in the intestines of sperm whales. It is a substance that prevents wounds whales receive from the sharp beaks and stings of giant squid, upon which they feed, from becoming infected. Ambergris, always a valuable substance, was, and still is, used to make perfumes.

At that time there were countless whales in the Moray Firth. Indeed, islands north of the Moray Firth were called the Orkneys, a name derived from the Latin, 'orca', a whale because of the vast number of whales, many of them sperm whales, in the surrounding waters. When the whales died, tides washed their dead bodies ashore, which then rotted on many beaches of the Moray Firth. Ambergris is extremely reluctant to decay. Consequently, for these two reasons, comparatively large amounts of ambergris were to found on the Moray Firth shores at that time.

Amber and ambergris are related only in that both are washed up on beaches. Amber is a fossilized resin from trees that grew in very ancient times. It was prized by people in the ancient world because, when rubbed, it attracts objects to it. This mysterious peculiarity, they thought, enabled it to cure certain diseases. The Greeks called it 'Elecktron'.

Amber was, and still is, found on the shores of the Baltic Sea at Jutland. There were three ancient amber routes from there. One was to the east, and two to the south; one of which was via the Moray Firth, then across the Highlands by way of Strath Bran and Glen Carron to the Sound of Sleat, and thence southwards on the Atlantic coast trade route through the Irish Sea to the Mediterranean.

The Picts were a Celtic people who are believed to have inhabited the western Highlands and Islands at that time. They differed from most other Celts in Scotland in that they had boats and regular contact with the Celts in Ireland, Wales; and Cornwall. This was especially true of the Celts in Cornwall firstly, because Arthur and Merlin, two early heroes held in common, are said to have been active in both places, and, secondly, because many Celtic saints, such as St Brandon, St Patrick, St Finbarr, St Néctan, and St Ninian, to mention but a few, passed backward and forward between the Picts and Cornish. From this, it follows that the Picts of the Iron Age must have had annual contact with the Mediterranean peoples who came to Britain.

It was the Picts who crossed the mainland by way of Glen Carron and Strath Bran, and undertook regular local voyages along the shores of the Moray Firth. Until the time of the Vikings, these voyages were sailed in daylight and only with fair wind. Come evening, the boats would be run ashore, to be launched on the day with a fair wind to continue the voyage. The beaches on the south shores of the Moray Firth have changed since those times and now are, in the main, stony. At that time every landing place had a sandy beach; and almost every one had a well on the shore above high water, especially made to provide water for voyagers.

When the Massiliotes no longer came because of Julius Cæsar's destruction of the Venetii merchant ships, neither did the iron-smiths bringing imported iron. The western Amber Route to the Mediterranean fell into disuse. However, at about this time, iron, ready for working, was discovered in the peat bogs.

It so happens that Scotland has no commercially workable iron seams because, in the past, glaciers had crushed the iron-bearing rocks beneath them pulverising into powder what mineral deposits there were in the strata, scattering them far and wide over the landscape. No iron veins have ever been discovered in the Highlands, other than deposits at Loch Maree, worked in antiquity, and a two-metre wide iron vein at Arndilly House, near Rothes in Banffshire, which may have been worked at the surface.

Iron can be produced in peat bogs. For this to happen, their waters at first need to be slightly acidic and contain very small amounts of dissolved oxygen near the surface. In this environment, a chemical reaction takes place precipitating insoluble iron compounds into the water. Anaerobic bacteria living below the surface concentrate iron as part of their living processes, forming pea-sized nodules of what is called 'bog iron'. This iron may be harvested from the same site once in a person's lifetime. Those small iridescent oily films one may notice on the surface of a bog show the presence of this kind of bacteria.

By the time the Pictish people had discovered 'bog iron' they had learned from the travelling iron-smiths how to use a furnace and, because of the high temperatures needed, how necessary it is that the charcoal used should be made from hard woods such as oak.

Smelting sites using 'bog-iron' are called 'bloomeries'. Many such sites have been found scattered about the countryside especially in Nairnshire, now part of Morayshire. The most recent of these bloomeries dates from the 1600's, the oldest from about 100 BC. All are on high ground where stronger winds increase the draught in the furnace. Making workable iron from bog-iron was time-consuming and the production low. No trace of 'bloomeries' has been found in Banffshire, which may be because there was never much hardwood forest hereabouts.

CHAPTER 6
FOUR ANCIENT TRACKWAYS

With sea trade passing along the south coast of the Moray Firth on the Amber Route, it is to be expected there would be long distance trackways from its shores to large settlements inland. The early Christian missionaries, following the Picts, passed this way and penetrated into this hinterland by way of the seven long-distance trackways, one from each of the following places: Portsoy, Whitehills, Banff, Macduff (Doune), Pennan, Gardenstown (Gamrie), and New Aberdour.

All the place-names that follow are Celtic; their translations into English are those of W. J. Watson or of J. Milne. In passing, it should be said that, with the exception of some river names, the oldest place-names in Britain and Europe are Celtic. This language, older than Latin, was spoken all over Europe before it disintegrated into sub-languages; surviving notably as the Gaelic of the Scottish, the Erse of the Irish, the Gymraeg of the Welsh, and Breiz the language of the Bretons. Elsewhere it has disappeared from everyday use, excepting for place-names which remain, usually as descriptions of the terrain. For instance, in the Grampian there is a place called Colpy ('copan' = small hill), a Meikle Colp, and the Hill of Colp a kilometre east of Turriff. There is a Colpy in Spain. And again, in the Grampian there is a Kemnay (a variant of 'caman' = 'place at a little crook in the river'), and a Kemnitz in Germany. There are rivers named Don in Britain and also a great river in Ukraine (Celtic 'U' = the/of + 'kraine' = green/grain) called the Don, though some say that name is pre-Celtic.

To return to the subject of ancient trackways, the one from Doune and the other from Gamrie are of special interest. Each led directly from the coast to the larger settlements of Picts at Bennachie. Each passed close to Balmellie Crofts, the oldest part of Turriff, where St Congan is said to have established a cell.

THE GAMRIE TRACKWAY started at Gamrie ('geamrachadh' = winter feeding, prepared seaweed for cattle and sheep; more likely from 'cam' = crooked + 'ruigh' = hill slope), now known as Gardenstown. It passed seven kilometres to the east of Balmellie Crofts, to which it was connected by a minor trackway.

From Gamrie it led through Dubford ('dubh' = muddy + 'ford'), then past

THE ROUTES OF FOUR VERY ANCIENT TRACKWAYS IN N.E. SCOTLAND

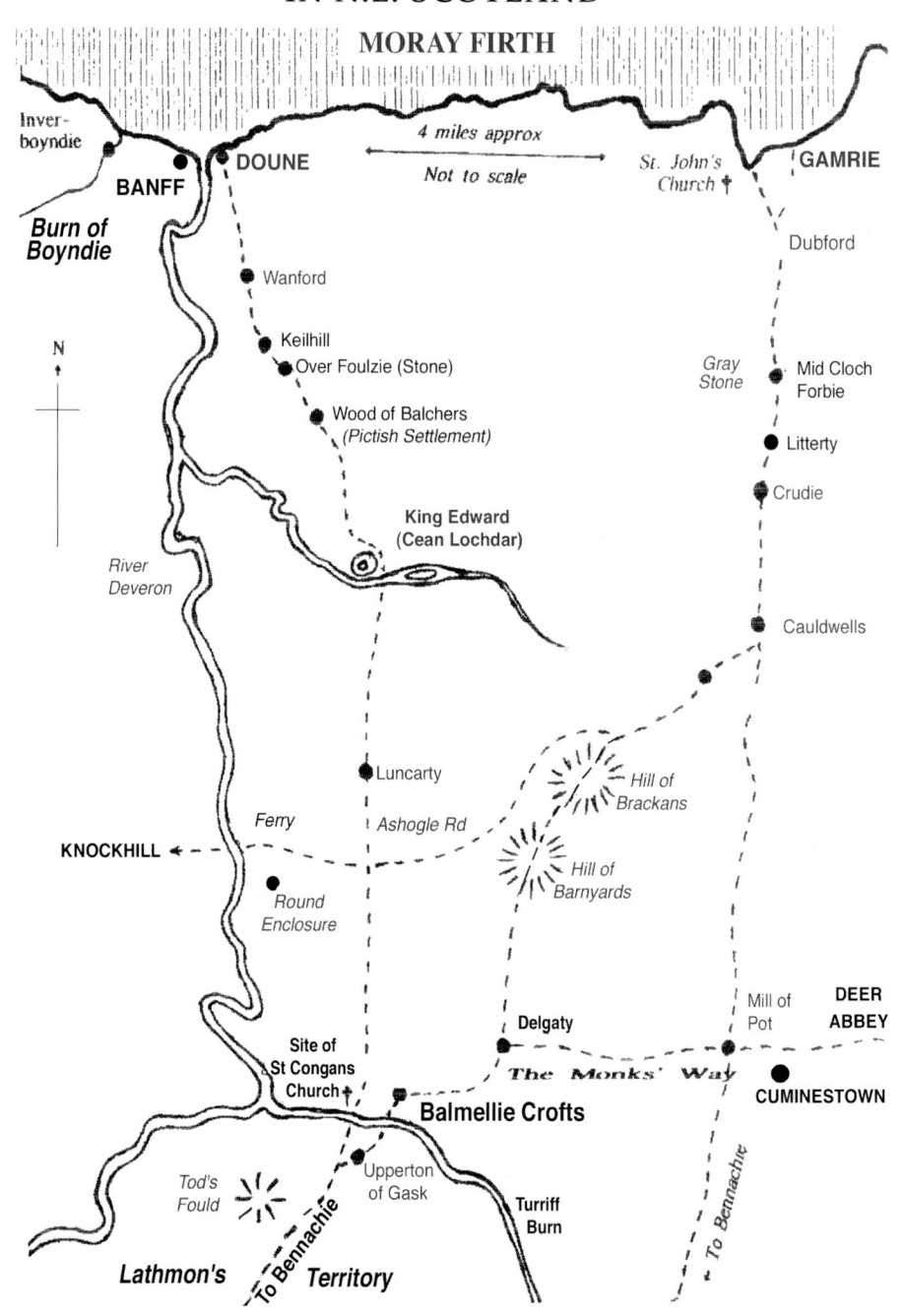

the monolithic grey stone at Mid Cloch Forbie ('cloch' = stone + 'forbie' = variant of 'ban' = white), thence through Crudie (place of judgement), Cauldwells, Cuminestown, and Fyfie ('croit chuithann' = croft of the small fold).

South of Cauldwells, this trackway divided. The way south led to Mill of Pots and thence to Bennachie. The way to the west led to Balmellie Crofts (Turriff) through Litterty ('Leitirtean' = hillsides), to Cotburn ('cuit' = cattle fold + burn), then southwards over the Hill of Brackans ('braighan' = little hill, the 's' has been added), and then over the Hill of Barnyard ('bearna' = a gap), to Delgaty ('dail' = field + 'goathach' = windy). It would appear from an inspection of the land at Delgaty that the name referred to a natural clearing amidst bog and forest, one of the earliest to be cultivated. This field would be one of several assarts, that is cultivated ground won from natural clearings in the wilderness; land that had to lie fallow for a year or more at a time, otherwise it would produce no further crop.

Delgaty and Balgreen ('bal' settlement + 'green' = grain, the cereal) it would seem, were two of the earliest assarts where cultivation first took place hereabouts, not forgetting the Bere Haugh ('bere' = barley + 'haugh' = hock, land in the shape of an animal's lower leg), beside the river Deveron below the site at the stone-age settlement at Dunlugas.

The 'windy field' in question once occupied the valley between the hill on which Delgaty Castle stands and the hill, at present wooded, opposite to the east. The terrain there is such that the air is rarely still. The field is no more. Where it was is now a lake.

Some say that after Waterloo, the last major battle of the Napoleonic Wars, homeless soldiers were encamped here and put to work making this lake; preparing the field, building a dam, and commencing a salmon ladder from the Turriff Burn. At the north end of the newly-formed lake, they built a stone bridge that bears the date 1815. After the work was completed, these ex-soldiers were dispersed to crofts roundabout, several of which bear the name 'Waterloo'. These are marked as such on the Ordnance Survey map.

There is an Iron Age relic at the water's edge on the east side of Delgaty lake; the small Lady Well ('laithen' = milk + 'well'), a place in the open where cows are milked in the summer. The French word 'lait', meaning milk, is derived from 'laithen'. This well has a surround of flat stones. The lake makes the well pointless. However, at the time when it was made on the spring-line, at the edge of a natural clearing suitable for grazing cows, it gushed with clear water. Once agriculture began at Delgaty, this clearing became a way-point for an existing trackway on which a settlement developed.

THE DOUNE TRACKWAY ('doun', a variant of 'dun' = a fort surrounded by a ditch) left the coast, following the east bank of the River Deveron, rising gradually to higher ground by way of Wansford ('wans' = cattle fold + ford) to Keilhill ('cuille' = little nook + English 'hill'), thence to Over Foulzie (a much corrupted Celtic word meaning cattle fold at a pool or burn, where there was a Stone).

From there, the trackway led through a large settlement, dating from Neolithic to Pictish times at the top of the highest hill hereabouts, now known as the Wood of Balchers ('baile chroise' = farm town at the crossroads). This settlement had three minor tracks leading to the Deveron, a kilometre away, one by way of Castle Eden. The Doune trackway traversed the hill, descending via Waterslack from where it led on to the dun at King Edward ('cean iochdar' = the lower heads of a burn that has divided and rejoined itself).

The trackway still half-circles this isolated rock on which the Normans replaced a Pictish dun with their stone castle, of which there is little left. Much stone-robbing, especially for building the adjacent earlier 18th century bridge by which the trackway crosses the Burn of King Edward, has left little. After crossing the burn the trackway crosses the modern A947 road, not far from the later Castleton Bridge, and becomes a minor road that was once the ancient highway to Turriff. After passing Luncarty (probably derived from 'longartaibh' = hunting lodge) it crosses another ancient trackway known as the Ashogle Road (much corrupted 'aiseag' = ferry + 'lach' = place of) at Knockiemill Cottages. Next it descends a steep slope to a ford at the turn for the Delster quarry, where there is now a stone bridge. A hedge once marked an older and more direct way to this ford, but was uprooted in 2004. The present winding, uphill road from the burn crossing was made when carts came into use after the days of the packhorse.

A kilometre west of Balmellie Crofts, the trackway enters Turriff, to pass straight along what is now its main street and lead down the brae to the Turriff Haughs, crossing these diagonally to the place on the south bank of the Turriff Burn, later named Bridgend.

At that time this burn had yet to be ditched. The crossing would be wider and, in places, very muddy. There would be no bridge only a ford, or, perhaps a boat. From Bridgend the trackway led on to the Bennachie by way of Nether Lenshie ('leathann' = broad + 'sith' = seat or hill).

THE MONKS' WAY is a much later name for part of the trackway that connected the Doune and Gamrie trackways, by way of Balmellie Crofts.

Deer Abbey ('deer', a variant of 'duraich' = oaks) a Druid's sanctuary that may have been made over peaceably to Christian use, is to the east of the Gamrie trackway. Monks leaving Deer Abbey for Congan's church at either of the two sites at Balmellie Crofts would first cross the South Ugie Water and proceed to Maud. From there they would take to the high ground over the Hill of Corse Gight ('crasg' = crossing + 'gaothach' = windy) to Mill of Pot, (north of the site of the later Cuminestown). There they would cross the Gamrie-Bennachie trackway to walk the four and a half kilometres or so, by way of Castle of Auchry (place on a slope) and Lambtech ('lamh' = hill + 'teach' = house), to Delgaty; twenty-three kilometres, a day's walk from Deer.

From Delgaty Castle the track of the Monks' Way followed what is now an ancient lane leading past the Delgaty Estate Farm Buildings, distinguished by a splendid bas-relief of the Greek god Dionysius above the entrance to the farm yard on the north side. A few metres beyond the Estate Buildings this well-defined lane comes to an abrupt end, the route lost over fields until, nearly at Balmellie Crofts, it becomes well-defined. Another minor track, well-defined at first, follows the east side of the lake. This also may have led to Balmellie Crofts.

From here, the trackway, no longer the Monks' Way, descended into the Turriff Haughs. It crossed the Turriff Burn at the site of the present, small wooden bridge, reputed to be part of an ancient right of way through Millmoss. From here it led up the hill to Upperton of Gask ('gasg' = a long narrow tail of land), to join the Doune-Bennachie trackway half a kilometre further to the west. From there it led to Nether Lenshie and on to the settlements at Bennachie.

THE ASHOGLE ROAD ('ashogle' = a variant of 'aiseag' pronounced 'ash' = ferry + 'lach' = 'place of', or according to W.J.Watson's probably correct derivation, 'rye ford') was once a trackway probably coming from east of Cauldwells. From there it led to Fintry and then St John's Well, continuing by way of the later field boundaries set along it in a line below the Hill of Brackens, to Meikle (big) and Little White Rashes (white' = 'chuit' = cattle fold + 'rashes' = 'ruighean' = slope of a hill). It leads past Wrae, along a minor road to cross a railway cutting, after which it descends through a ravine and thence by way of an overgrown metalled road to the left bank of the River Deveron. Here until recent times, there was a ferry, the Boat of Ashogle. From the left bank of the

Deveron, the trackway crossed the Forglen estate to Aberchirder and thence, probably, to Knock Hill.

Barbara's Hillock is at the Tillyfar turn, on the Turriff/Dunlugas road near the place where the Ashogle trackway crosses it. This is a prominent, natural grass-covered, round hill, not unlike a tumulus, within which a stone age coffin containing human remains was found in 1850.

An Iron-Age enclosure is to be found east of the Ashogle trackway where it approaches the right bank of River Deveron. This kind of Round was used as a fold for cattle prior to moving them across the Deveron. The British Celts were renowned in Europe as successful cattle breeders and they moved herds, often, for great distances. There are many places in Britain that have similar iron-age cattle folds adjacent to rivers for this purpose.

CHAPTER 7
THE CHURCHS AND CHAPELS OF ST CONGAN

St Congan lived in the first half of the 8th Century AD, first in Ireland, then in the Islands and Highlands, and finally in the East of Scotland. He was a Celtic monk, a Culdee, which just means 'a man of God'. He preached, as was the practice of Culdee monks, at fords, wells, and springs; in fact anywhere where people were on the move, especially in summer at landing-places on the seashore. It would seem that, as did St Brendon the Voyager, St Congan travelled trade routes intentionally. Once he had built a church or chapel he would move on, leaving behind a monk from his entourage to continue preaching the gospel and proselytizing.

The Kalendars of Scottish Saints, as quoted by W. J. Watson, credit St Congan with establishing his churches and chapels [Cill Chomhghain = 'Kilchoan' (pronounced 'kil-who-an') = 'Church of Comgan'] on twelve sites, all in the north of Scotland. They appear first in the following list in the order given in the Kalendars:

1. Kilchoan in Islay,
2. Kilchoan in Ardnamurchan,
3. Kilchoan on Loch Melfort in Argyll,
4. Lochalsh in Wester Ross,
5. Kilchoan in Glendale in Duirninish,
6. Kilchoan in Kilbrandon on Seil,
7. Kilchoan in Knoydart,
8. Kilchowan in Kiltearn Parish (now called Mountrich, in Easter Ross),
9. Kilchoan, (changed in the Middle Ages to 'Teampull Chaoin' = Comgan's Temple), at Boreraig on Loch Eishort in Skye,
10. Kilchoan (a chapel) in Lumlair,
11. St. Coan in Strath,
12. Turriff, Aberdeenshire,
13. Teampuill Chaon at Ord on Loch Eishort in Skye,
14. Cladh Chomhghain = 'Comgan's Cemetery' in North Uist.

The 13th and 14th churches are not mentioned in the Kalendars of Scottish Saints, but are recorded by the Royal Commission on the Ancient and Historic Monuments of Scotland (RCAHMS).

W.J.Watson says there may have been other Congan churches if only because the name MacGille Comgain (son of St Comgan's servant) was long found in Dingwall and also in Argyll, and that there was a Gille Chomghgain, a Mormaer (High Steward) of Moray, who died in 1032. He also says Kirkcowan in Wigtown does not commemorate St Congan, but a St. Eogan.

SCOTLAND
The Western Amber Route to the Mediterranean
and the sites of
St Congan's Churches and Chapels
(Not contemporaneous)

The Amber Route
From Jutland

LEGEND

1. Cill Chomhan near Port Asabuis, Islay
2. Kilchoan in Ardnamurchan
3. Kilchoan on Loch Melford in Argyll
4. Kirkton, Lochalsh in Wester Ross
5. Kilchoan in Glendale in Duirninish, Skye.
6. Kilchoan in Kilbrandon on Seil
7. Kilchoan in Knoydart.
8. Kilchowan in Kiltearn Parish near Dingwall. (now called Mountrich, in Easter Ross).
9. Kilchoan, "Teampuill Choan" on Loch Eishort, at Boreraig in Skye.
10. Kilchoan (a chapel) in Lumlair, Cromarty Firth.
11. St Coan at Trumpan, in Strath, Waternish, Skye
12. Turriff Aberdeenshire
13. Kilchoan, 'Teampuill Chaoin' on Loch Eishort, at Ord, Sleat, Skye.
14. Cladh Chotain ('Comgan's Cemetery'), in North Uist.

Iona

To the Mediterranean

From the maps below it can be seen that all except one of St Congan's chapel sites are at landing places regularly used by Picts travelling between the islands and along the coast. Four of the chapel sites listed below are marked with asterisks. These chapel or church sites are significant because they are at landing places at the ends of the overland route between the Moray Firth and the Atlantic. In St Congan's time the Amber Route was defunct, although of course the landing places on it were used by the Picts.

Remains of buildings on the sites mentioned are post-Congan and of mediaeval origin. Definitions of place-names are from the Celtic unless otherwise mentioned.

1. *Cill Chomhan on Islay.*

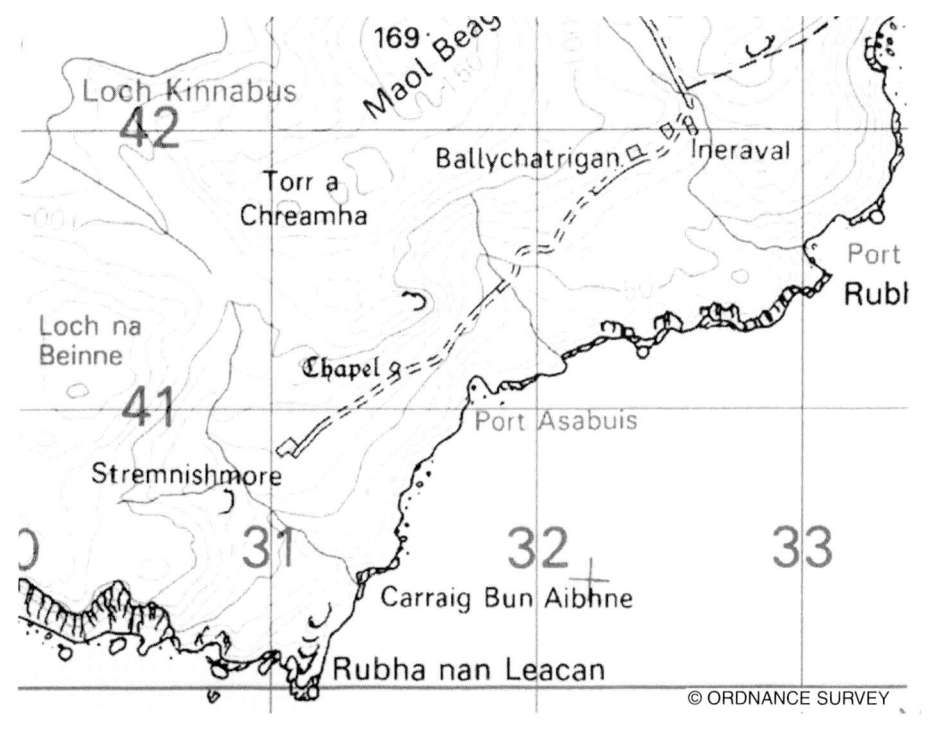

If the name Islay is to be derived from the Celtic, it may be compared with the Gaulish 'ilio-maros', meaning 'big-buttocked', which might well describes the proportions of the island as viewed from the south. This kind of association is in keeping with Celtic practice; often they referred to a long, narrow piece of land as a 'haugh' (hock), the word used to describe the lower leg of a carcass. However, a derivation from the Welsh verb 'ilio', meaning 'ferment', is perhaps more pertinent considering the number of distilleries on the island. Ptolemy the map-maker (AD 100 - c.178) called the island Epidion.

This site of a chapel dedicated to St Congan is on a south-facing hillside about 300m west of the boat-landing at Port Asabuis at map reference OS sheet 60 (1)314 (6)412. There are traces here of a very early settlement.

Kilchoman, near the landing beach of Tràigh Mhachir, at map reference OS Sheet 60 (1) 216 (6)631, has nothing to do with St Congan being an earlier foundation dedicated to a St Comman, (of whom there were several of that name), who died in 688. [RCAHMS, Argyll Inventory of Monuments Vol.5].

2. *Kilchoan on Ardnamurchan.*

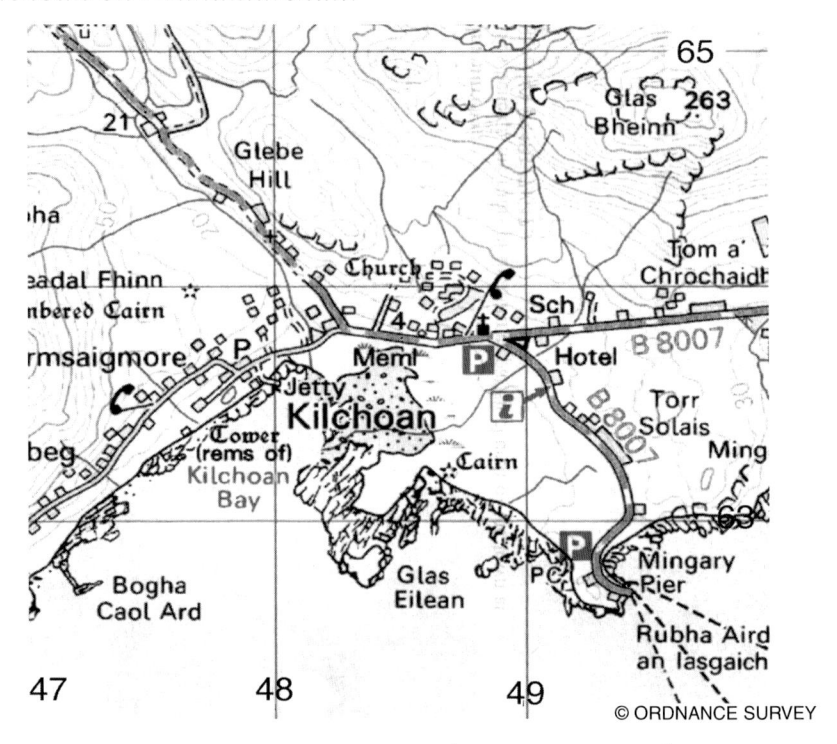

There are several derivations for Ardnamurchan. 'Ard na murchon' = 'Point of the Sea-hounds' (otters); 'Attda Muirchol' = 'Capes of Sea-Sins' (places of piracy and wrecking). St Columba is recorded as having met sailors from Ireland whilst walking on the strand at Ardnamurchan.

St Congan's chapel lies beneath the ruins of the former parish church of the town at map reference OS Sheet 47 (1)482 (7)641.

3. *Kilchoan on Loch Melford in Argyll.*

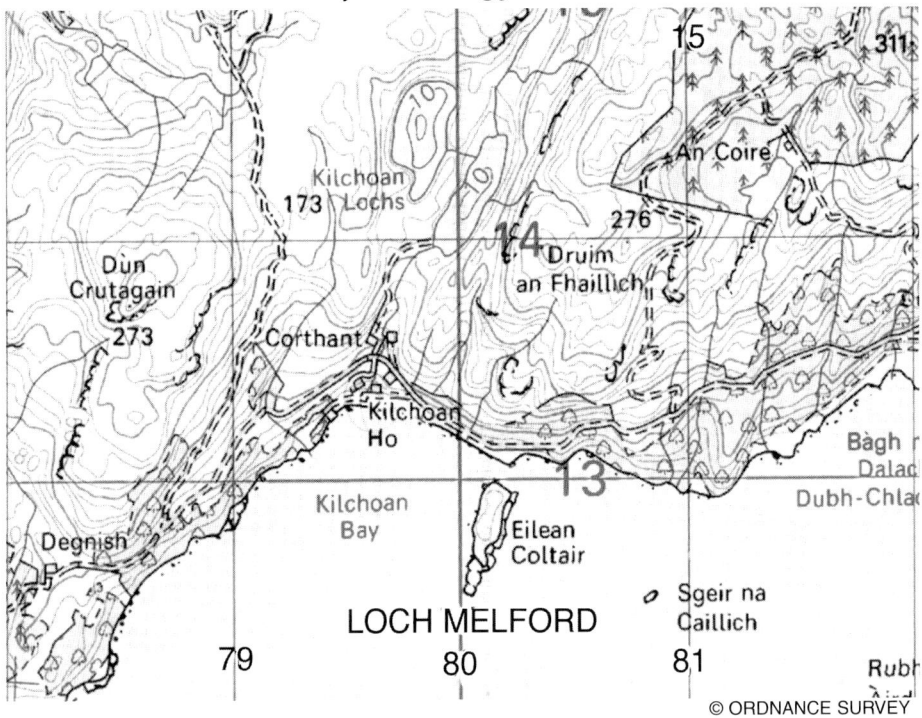

Melfort may be derived from 'maol' = 'bare' + 'fort', a corruption of 'port', meaning a landing place with little shelter.

Kilchoan House, at map reference OS Sheet 55 (1)796 (7)134, is built upon the site of a chapel called Kilcongen, which, according to a charter of 1313, was dedicated to St Congan.

Kilchoan Lochs, one kilometre further north, at map references OS Sheet 55 (7)798(1)145 & (7)800(1)142, are remembered because they must have been places where St Congan performed baptisms.

*4. Kirkton at Lochalsh near the Kyles of Lochalsh.

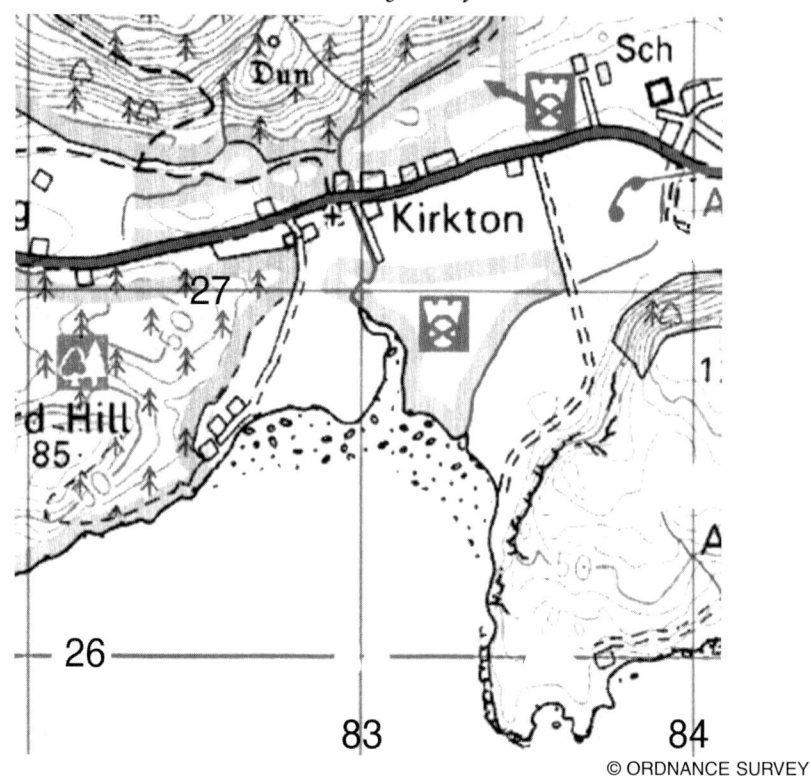

© ORDNANCE SURVEY

The derivation of Lochalsh is uncertain. The most likely is 'loch', a lake + 'aillseach', meaning sweaty, referring to foam and scum on the water, not unlike that which forms on the necks and under the saddles of hard-ridden horses.

St Congan's church lies near or beneath a modern church building dedicated to him, at map reference OS sheet 33 (1)829 (8)273. It was sited above an important ancient landing beach, now the property of the Scottish National Trust, and was the Atlantic end of the Amber route overland from the Cromarty Firth.

5. *Kilchoan in Glen Dale, Duirinish, Skye.*

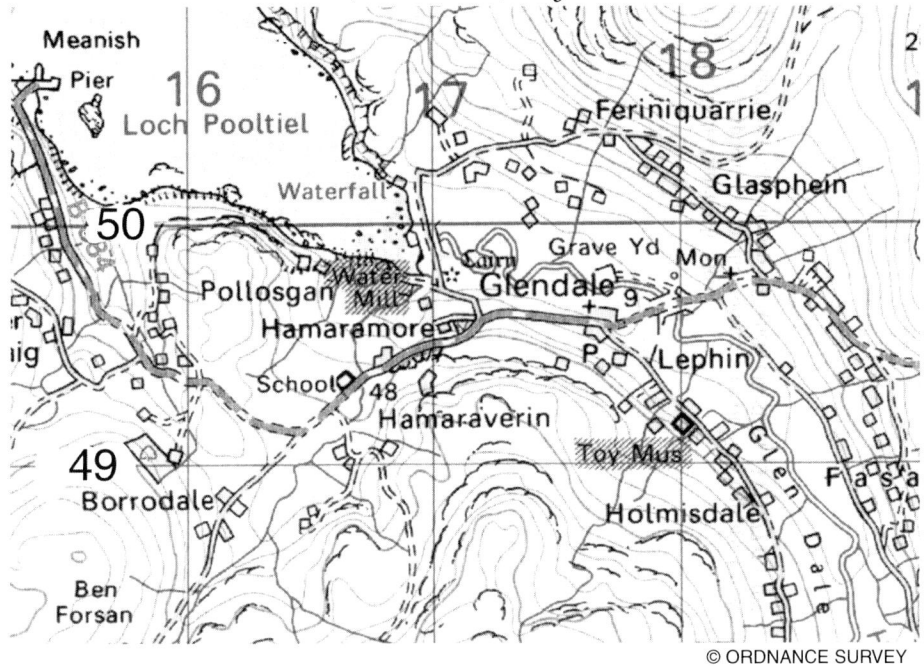

The derivation of Skye is a complicated matter. The name currently in use comes from St Admanan who wrote 'Scia insula', which he may have taken from the Celtic 'skitis', meaning 'divided'; hence the 'Divided Isle' or 'Winged Isle'.

'Durinish' means 'little black point', which aptly describes the appearance of this place at the end of Loch Pooltiel where narrow Glendale passes between high mountains, as seen from seaward.

A graveyard near Glasphein is on the former site of St Congan's Church 0.75 kilometres from a landing beach, at map reference OS Sheet 23 (1)177 (8) 498. There is a local tradition that a Danish prince named Cuon is buried here. He perished in Meanish Bay whilst on a raiding trip to the Western Isles. 'Meanish' may be from 'min' = 'smooth' + the diminutive 'ish' which must refer to the tiny sheltered area of smooth water between the west shore and an islet, immediately south of the present pier. Probably this legend was invented to explain the name after Congan had been forgotten [Compare 'Cuan' at Seil Island at 6 below].

6. Kilchoan in Kilbrandon on Seil Island.

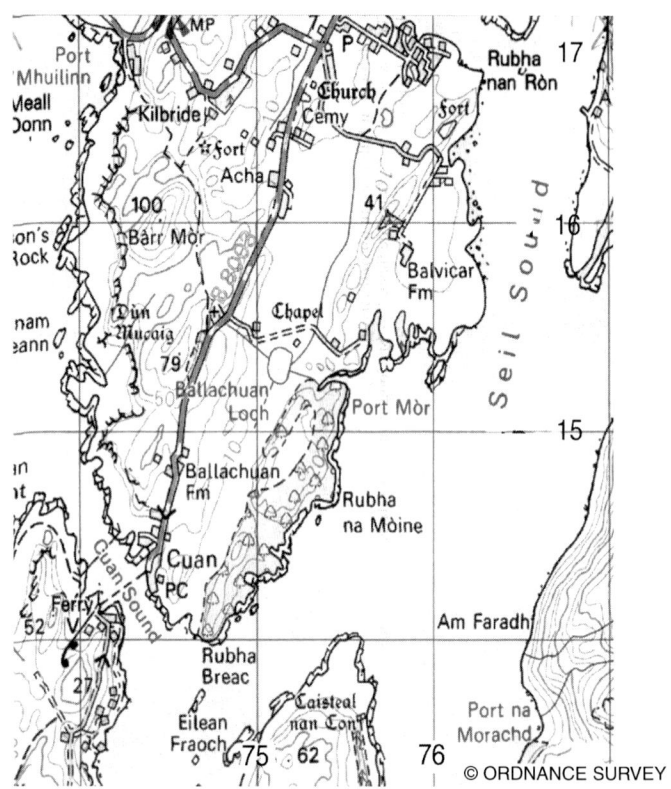

[Map excerpt © ORDNANCE SURVEY showing Seil Island area including Port Mhuilinn, Kilbride, Barr Mòr, Balvicar Fm, Ballachuan, Cuan Sound, Ferry, Rubha Breac, Eilean Fraoch, Caisteal nan Con, Port na Morachd, and Seil Sound.]

There is a chapel site dedicated to St Brandon at map reference OS Sheet 55 (1)752 (7)154. The Kalendars say there was a Kilchoan on Seil and that St Congan built a chapel here. At times, he seems to have been following in the wake of St Brandon the Voyager, who sailed the trade routes, and must have visited the parish named after him near Banff, on his way to Turriff.

The inshore route between the Shuna and Seil Sounds is a waterway of the greatest antiquity. People from the chiefdoms of Strathclyde making for the Highlands would portage their boats, usually curachs, always hide-sided, across the Kintyre peninsula at Tarbert ('tairbeart' = 'an overbringing', a portage between seas). From Tarbert they would sail waters protected from the open Atlantic by the isles of Jura, Luing and Seil to Oban and its natural harbour sheltered by the isle Kerrera. From Oban, they would take either the sheltered waters of Loch Linne to Fort William, or, north-westwards, to Ardnamurchan through the Sound of Mull, then through the Sound of Sleat, Skye, for Lochalsh; and thence to the north. Much later, this route, excepting for the portage, was once taken by 'puffers', the steam coasters of Glasgow.

The chapel site is beside the tiny Ballachuan Loch which is fed by a burn. A short distance to the northeast of this loch is a convenient area of flat land upon which, since the Stone Age, there has been settlement after settlement. A few metres away is Port Mór on Seil Sound, an ancient landing place where once ships on passage were beached by their crews who no doubt traded with those living nearby, whilst awaiting a favourable wind or tide.

The Book of Leinster and the monk, St Adamnan (624 - 704), record an expedition from the monastery at Hí (Iona) to Sóil (Seil), in 568, for oaks to repair the Abbey. It is worth noting that to transport an oak trunk whole, or as planks, requires a sizeable curach of some ten metres or more, made of cow-hide stretched over the wooden frame, the keel, and gunwales.

Skene identifies Sóil as this particular burn. Admanan dignifies it with the name 'river', saying his companions caught salmon there without nets. The name is pre-Celtic with no remembered meaning, as is the river Sale, a tributary to the Moselle in Germany, and the river Soar in Leicestershire. The modern form in Gaelic is 'Seile', and is taken to mean 'sail', but that could not be its original meaning. Apart from the burn at Seil, two more rivers in Scotland have the same name, the Sheil of Moidart and the Sheil at the head of Loch Duich.

It would seem then, that the whole of Seil took its name from the burn at the only settlement. The nearby Ballachoan Loch received its name because it was near 'St Congan's settlement ('bal an Choan') and he used it for baptisms, as he did the lochs named after him at Melfort.

Cuan, a place on the shore of Cuan Sound from whence a ferry crosses to Luing Isle, is at map reference OS Sheet 55 (1)754 (7)144. There is a Cuan Point on the isle of Luing ('luing' = a 'boat with sail'). All three place-names may refer to St Congan even though 'cuan' is the Gaelic for 'sea' or 'ocean', a conflation that may have occurred after the saint had become a memory hereabouts. One of the early manuscripts mentions him as Coan: which compare with the legend of 'Cuon', a Danish Prince, drowned at Kilchoan Glendale, Skye (See 5 above).

7. Kilchoan in Knoydart.

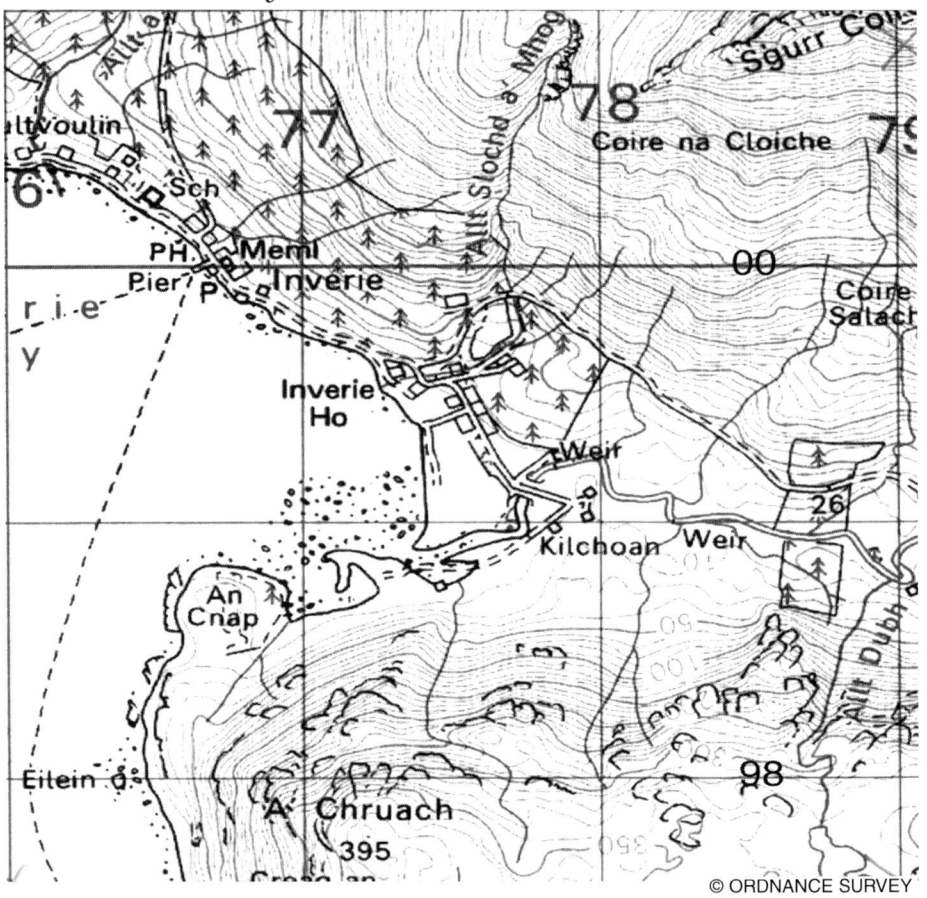

Sir Herbert Maxwell in his 'Scottish Landnames' says Knóydart comes from the Norse 'Cnut's Firth'. Dwelly's Gaelic Dictionary says the name is from the Celtic 'knoideart', which may mean 'splendid place'. The beautiful and sheltered River Dart in Devon may have been called 'Knoideart'.

The site of St Congan's church is a kilometre SE of the pier at Inverie at Knoydart within a bend of the Inverie River, north of a place called Kilchoan, at map reference OS Sheet 33 (1)779 (7)991. There are three graveyards nearby.

*8. Kilchowan in Kiltearn Parish, Easter Ross, now called Mountrich.

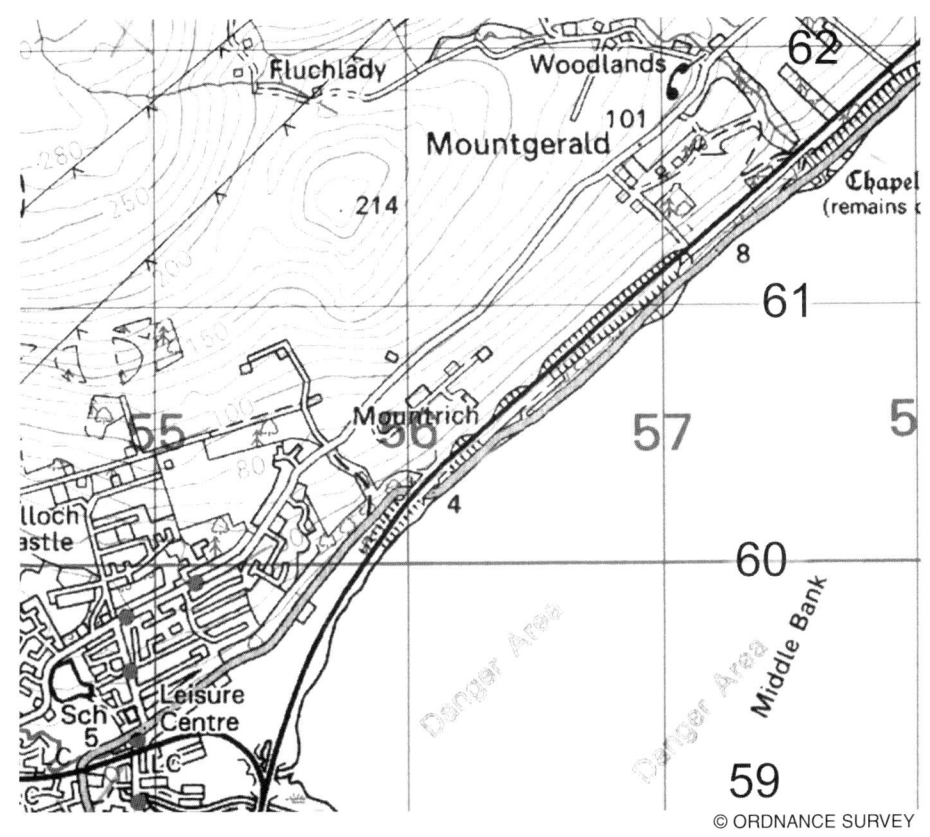

© ORDNANCE SURVEY

This place is associated with a chapel called Kilchoan at Lemlair nearby (See *10).

This chapel was at Mountrich ('monadh' = a hill pasture + 'righe' summer sheiling), near Dingwall. During the building of the railway in the 19th Century, the site was destroyed leaving no remains. However, there is a present-day St Congan's Cottage at map reference OS Sheet 21 (2) 559 (8) 606. [Note: Watson says the name MacGille Comgain (son of St Comgan's servant) was long found in this area].

This chapel and the one at Lemlair were at the North Sea end of the overland part of the Amber route that led to the beach at Kirkton, Lockalsh and the Atlantic (See *9).

Although Kiltearn means 'place of prayer' it may be a variant of Kilchowan.

*9. Kilchoan at Dun Boreraig, Skye.

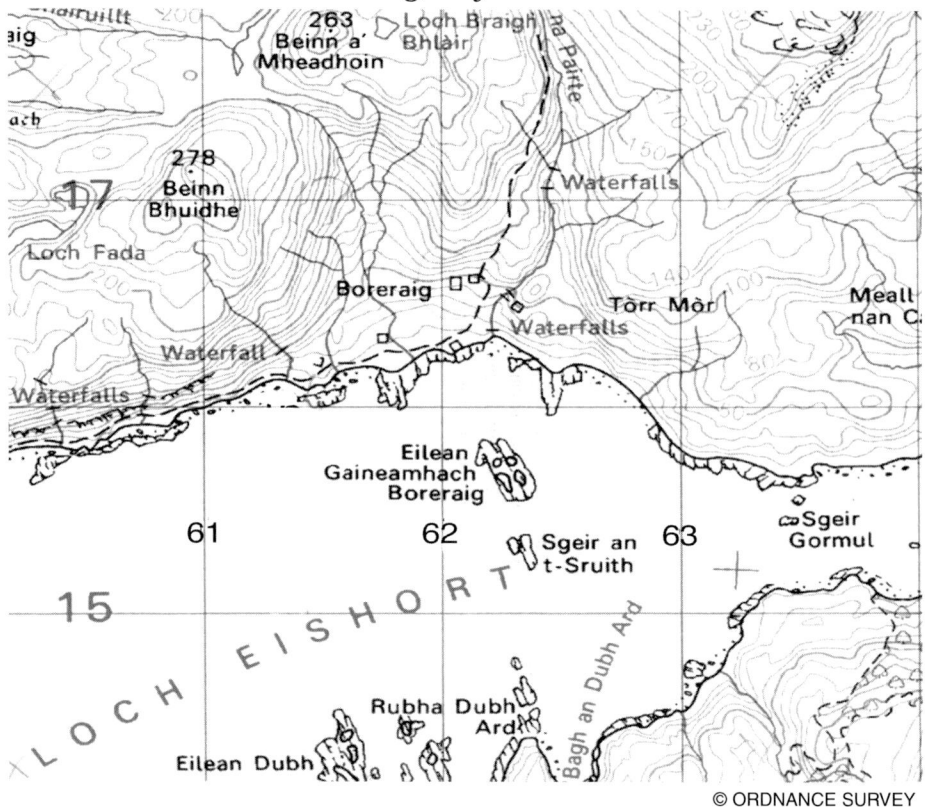

© ORDNANCE SURVEY

'Dun' is a Celtic word, meaning 'fortified hill', 'Boreraig' is Old Norse meaning 'bay', hence the 'burgh on the bay". The site of the mediæval church is on grassy level ground above the north shore of Loch Eishort, 328 metres ENE of Dun Boreraig, a Stone Age circle, within which St Congan is said to have built his church. The name was changed in the Middle Ages to 'Teampuill Choain' (Congan's Temple). Map reference of the later church is OS Sheet 32 (1)618 (8) 163.

This site is associated with Kilchoan at An t' Ord, Sleat, Skye (See *13).

*10. Kilchoan, a chapel in Lumlair (now called Lemlair) in Easter Ross.

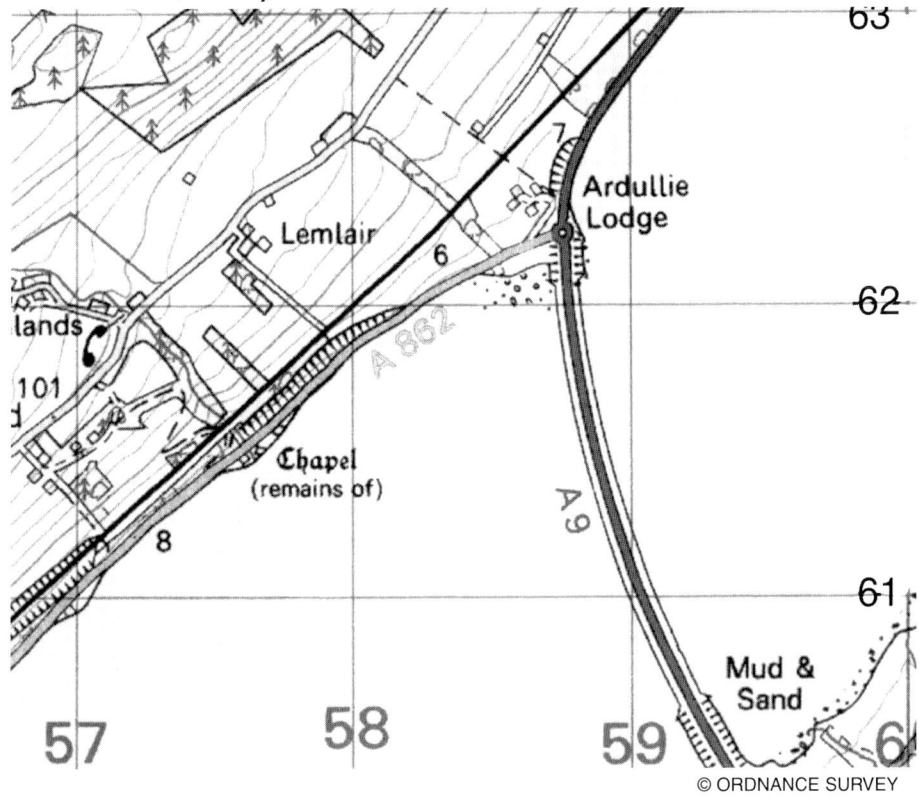

© ORDNANCE SURVEY

This is associated with a chapel at Kilchoan at Mountrich in Kiltearn Parish (See 8*).

The remains of a ruined chapel and a graveyard on the seashore near Castle Foulis are all that remains of the site at map reference OS Sheet 21 (2)576 (8) 615.

Lumlair, possibly derived from either 'lom' = bare + 'lair' = ground, or from the Welsh 'llan' + 'lair' meaning 'church ground'.

The evidence suggests this is the site of St Congan's Chapel. The Saint was soon forgotten here, it seems, and, because of the depredations of the sea, the place was given the name of Cille Bhrea (Cille = chapel + 'bhrea' derived from 'breaban' = 'anything hanging on to anything else'; in this case, to a building clinging to the beach). When the Roman church arrived, its monks rebuilt the chapel and dedicated it to St Mary, a name taken from the Church's list of approved saints, as was their practice.

The evidence, such as it is, suggests, in the time of the Mediterranean traders, this was the North Sea end and the beginning of the overland part of Amber route from Jutland to the beach at Kirkton, Lockalsh, and the Atlantic.

It would seem that the water level in the Firth of Cromarty varied. At the time of St Congan it was lower and the Firth deeper than now. The 'L' shape of the old sandbank immediately offshore suggests there was an harbour at this place, especially as a ferry had plied for centuries until quite recently from here to the opposite shore.

The varying levels in the Firth can be explained. Between 500 and 1000 AD, partly in the time of the coming of the Irish monks, there were perturbations of tides and sea levels around Britain and Brittany. There were sudden inundations of coasts at the western end of the English Channel and in the Irish Sea at the Gower peninsula, South Wales, which are on record. As well as in the Cromarty Firth, it would seem there were similar tidal fluctuations on the Moray coast at Burghhead, once known as the Isle of Bulls; and that Lossiemouth, previously an island, became connected with the mainland, though there are no written records.

There were parallel happenings. In the same period, the city of Yse on the Brittany coast was drowned in an inundation recorded in detail in the Lives of St Winwaloe and Gradlon, king of Yse. This happening passed into a legend that inspired Chaucer's evocative poem, 'The Franklin's Tale'. It was the source of inspiration for Eduarde Lalo when he was writing his opera 'Le Roi d'Ys', just as it was for Claude Debussy when he was composing his piano work, 'La Cathédrale Engloutie', the submerged cathedral.

These unexpected tidal perturbations happened on several occasions between the years 700 to 1000 AD. One such turned Godwin Island near the Straits of Dover into the Goodwin Sands. They must have made life difficult on the shoreline and were the reason that Cille Bhrea was abandoned in favour of a chapel built at Mountrich. After the tidal perturbations ceased the ferry still being in use, a mediæval chapel was built on the same site on the shore and dedicated to St Mary, as said above. Then, probably, the Mountrich chapel was abandoned. A lady living locally informed us that, in the 1970's, she used to take her children to play on the shore near this ruin at Lemlair, and often they found human bones protruding from the ground after gale-driven tides had reached and eroded the graveyard.

Latter-day silting, however, eventually reduced the landing place to a shallow strand. The ferry grounded each time it arrived. Passengers and cargo were being landed in the water. It became more than could be tolerated and the crossing was abandoned.

11. St Coan a chapel in Strath at Trumpan on Ardmore Bay, Waternish, Skye.

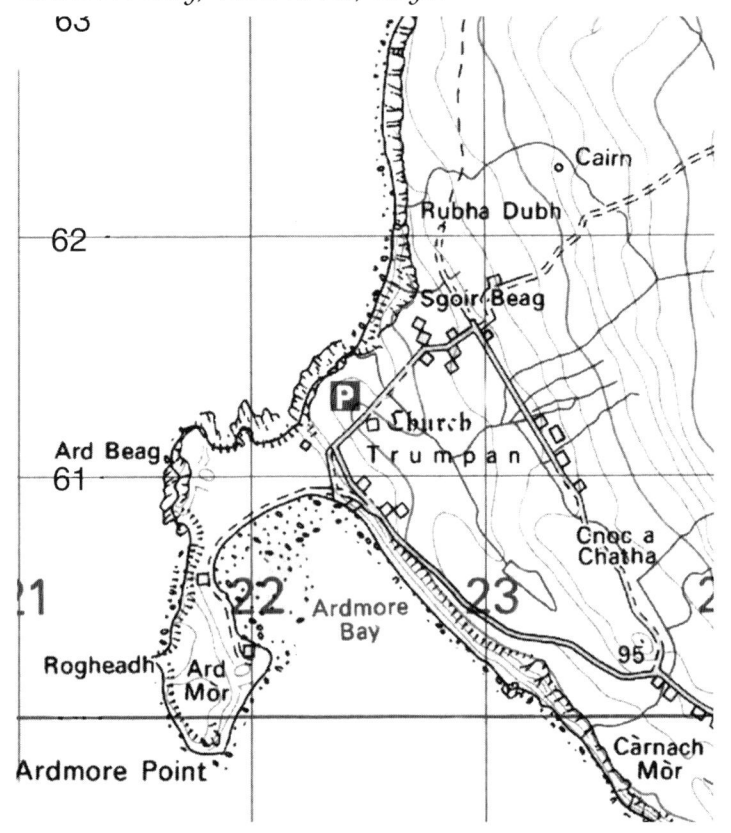

© ORDNANCE SURVEY

Trumpan may be an Old Norse word meaning 'one-sided hillock'. Ardmore, is from the Celtic 'An t-'Ard Mór' meaning 'the prominent height'. Waternish may be a corruption derived from 'bharraich', meaning 'small landing place' according to the entry in Dwelly's Gaelic Dictionary.

   A graveyard and the ruins of a mediæval church are on the site of St Congan's chapel 0.5 km from a good anchorage and landing place at Ardmore Bay, at map reference OS Sheet 23 (8)225 (6) 612.

12. Turriff, Aberdeenshire.

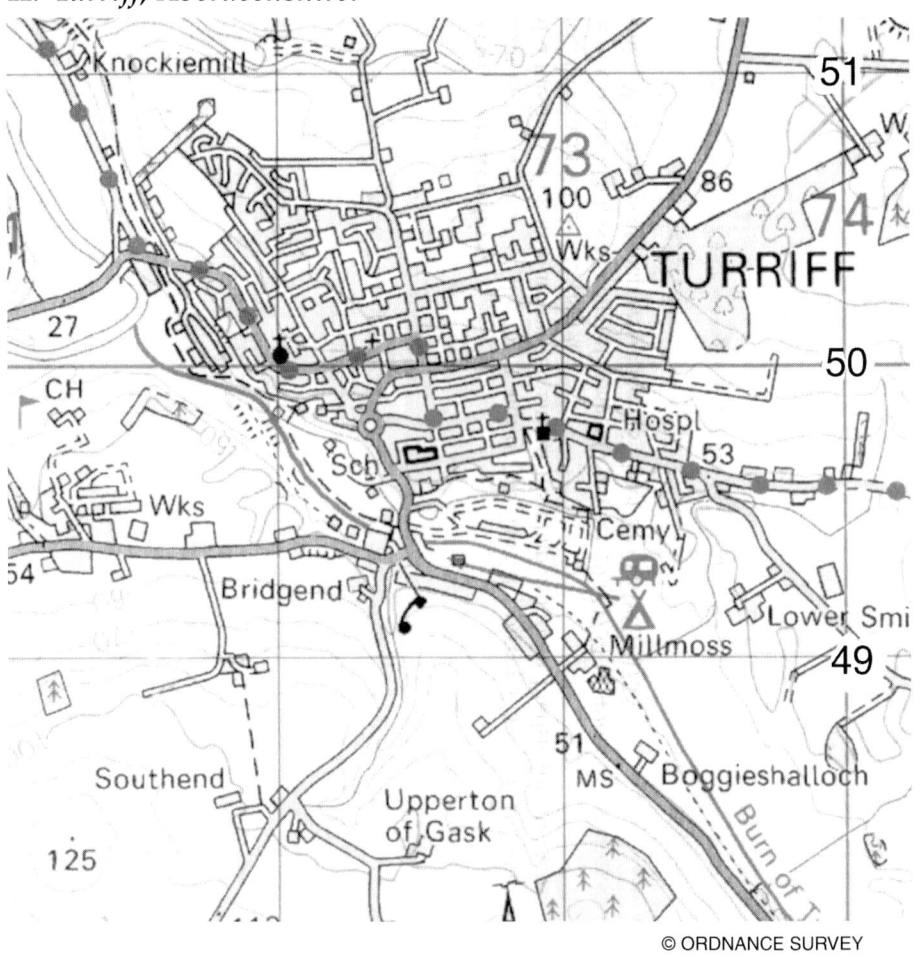

© ORDNANCE SURVEY

Turriff may be a variant of 'tor' = hill + 'Brude', a Pictish name, but more probably it is from an earlier time than that of Brude and is derived from 'tor' + 'rath', a 'round'.

St Congan is patron saint of the town and also of the Turriff Episcopalian Church. The site of his chapel on a Pictish fort where are the ruins of a mediaeval church is at map reference OS Sheet 29 (3)722 (8)498. The site of his Den is at map reference OS Sheet 29 (3)734 (8)496. The Monks' Way begins at map reference OS Sheet 29 (3) 735 (8)498. A full description of St Congan, his life and times, is given in Chapter 10.

*13. **Kilchoan at An t' Ord, Sleat, Skye.***

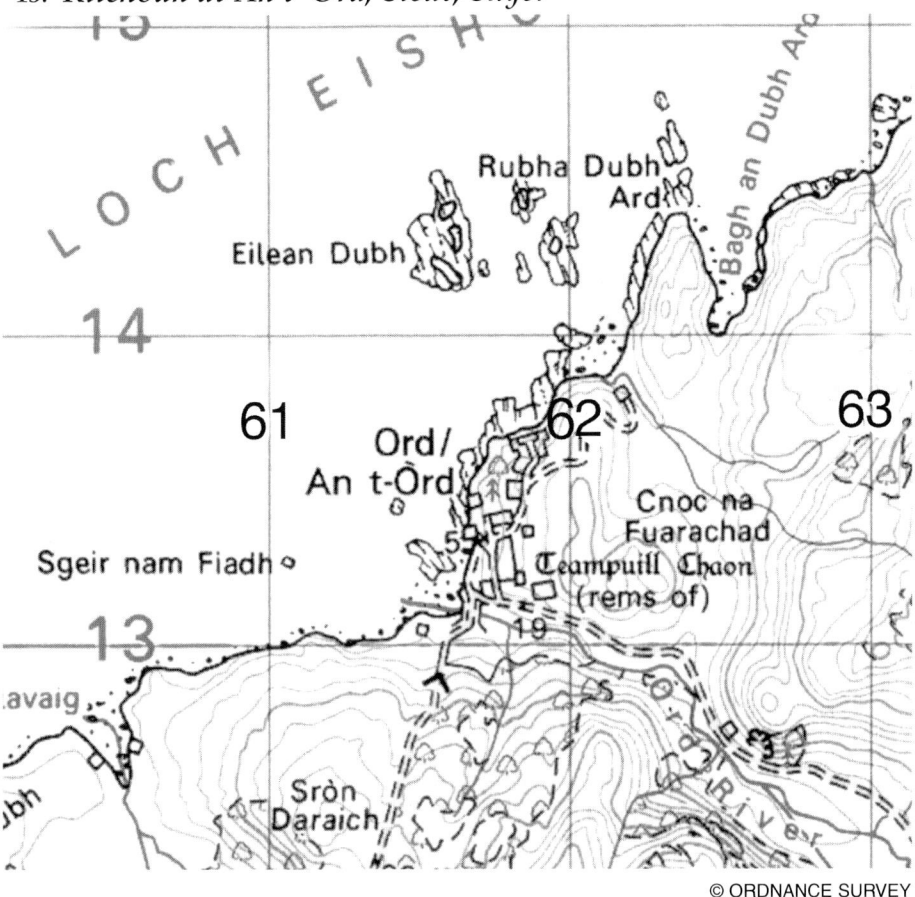

© ORDNANCE SURVEY

Án t' Ord' (the hammer), presumably named from the shape of the coastal prominence there as seen from the sea. 'Ord' is both an Old Celtic and an Old Norse word. Place names that are similar in Norse and Celtic often date back to when Old Celtic (the Gaelic) was spoken all over Europe, the younger Norse language being derived from Celtic.

'Teampuill Chaoin' (Congan's Temple), again, a name-change dating from the Middle Ages, is above the beach at Ord at map reference OS Sheet 32 (1)618(8)133. The site is recorded in the RCAHMS Argyll Inventory Vol. 5.

An t' Ord is associated with (*9) Kilchoan at Dun Boreraig. It is not mentioned in the Kalendar of Scottish Saints perhaps because the compilers presumed it was the same place as Dun Borereig (see*9), believing there could not be two chapels dedicated to St. Congan's on Loch Eisort.

These two ancient landing places, the one at Dun Boreraig and the other at Ord, are a double site, being two kilometres apart, opposite each other across Loch Eisort. In the time of the Atlantic Coast Trade, they were alternative landing places for Kirkton near Lockalsh, the gateway to the Atlantic for the ancient Amber Route that crossed Scotland at this latitude.

Any ship, prevented by a strong tide and a contrary wind from entering the Sound of Sleat and making its true destination of Lochalsh, as an alternative would steer for either of the two landings places in Loch Eisort, as the wind direction served. Should such a ship be forced to make Ord, once there the captain would await a fair wind to continue north to Dun Boreraig, which, when that wind came, usually meant that place was reached in less than an hour's sailing. From Dun Boreraig, the trader would continue his journey to Kirton-at-Lochalsh by land via Broadfoot, crossing to the mainland at Kyleakin, a much shorter and easier journey than that from Ord.

14. *Cladh Chotain* = 'Comgan's Cemetery', in North Uist.

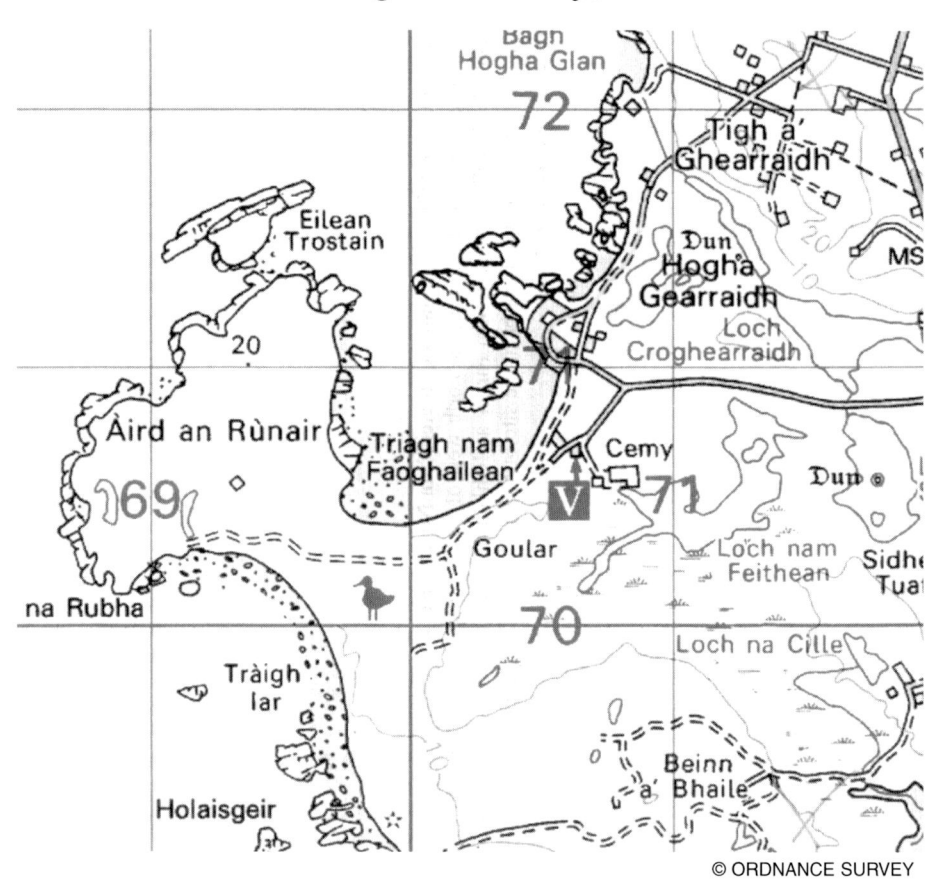

© ORDNANCE SURVEY

This burial site at Áird an Rùnair in the north west of Uist, at map reference OS sheet 69 (0)695 (8)706, was known earlier as Chladh Chomhghain, according to W. J. Watson. It is thought to have been the site of a chapel and burial ground of which no trace of either remains. A walled enclosure containing a group of small cairns was noted there in 1911 by W. Beveridge, who lived on the islet of Vallay, not far away. When visited by the Ordnance Survey in 1965, all the land was under plough. From this meagre history it may be that St Congan came here but never stayed.

Cladh Chotain is better known as the birth-place of John MacCodrum, the Bard of North Uist (1710 - 1796) because in a verse of his Gaelic poem, 'The Mavis of Clan Donald', he sings:

> "In Congan's Churchyard was I born, in Áird an Rúnnair I was reared, in sight of the proud throbbing sea, of the sportive, fickle, playful waves."

CHAPTER 8
BALMELLIE CROFTS

Fields on the east side of Turriff, once moorland on rising land beside the Balmellie Road, opposite the head of Cowan's Den, were known until recently as the Balmellie Crofts ('Bal' = town + 'mellie' = low hill; 'croit' = croft = a small piece of enclosed ground). They are now an housing estate served by Hatton Road, Mayfield Road, Ardin Road, and Roseacre Crescent.

The Celtic name, Ballmellie Crofts, implies a Pictish settlement; a conjecture re-inforced by the proximity of the Monks' Way, and the legend that St Congan (Cowan) is associated with the Den adjacent to the Crofts.

This Pictish settlement came into being when agriculture had begun to thrive in the district. As a settlement, it was not as old as the two coastal trackways, the one from Doune and the other from Gamrie, with which it was joined. The settlement, instead of being situated on one of them, fortuitously, is a short distance from each. It seems that the Picts, as did the people before them, chose the place for its generous supply of spring water, uniquely distributed.

Hearsay has it that until the beginning of the 19th century there had been a copious amount of water flowing down a burn that ran through Balmellie Crofts into Cowan's Den. It was said that before field drainage took place there were quite a few natural wells about the Crofts. Each had its own small brook to take the overflow either to the burn or to the Collie Stripe ('coille' = 'wood' + 'stripe' a NE Scottish variant of 'stream'), a hundred metres or so to the east.

When field drains were laid in the Crofts, a Mr Duff from Dufftown is quoted as saying the brooks from the wells were piped into the burn, which was enlarged as far as Cowan's Den. In time, this burn became a stone-built, covered culvert, above which yet another of earthen banks was made to take storm water.

A definition of a 'well' would not come amiss here. In earlier times, the water-table, that is the level on hillsides where springs occur, was very much higher everywhere in Britain than it is now. Wherever there were banks at this level, there were springs. On flat land, other than fenland, there being no banks, water 'welled' up from the soil. In such places, this 'living water' washed out holes and from which it overflowed. Indeed, to this present day there are three or four such wells within the Den itself. It would seem that those Picts living here kept each well in a separate enclosure, hence the term 'crofts'.

The reasons for a settlement being at the Balmellie Crofts are now apparent. The people there were taking advantage of a convenient, constant, and ample supply of clean running water for necessary industries. They practised water management in that water for drinking was taken from the well highest up the hill, it being the least likely to be polluted. If other places that have been researched are example, the wells in the lower crofts would have been used separately, one for beer-making, one with a pond for retting for flax and stinging nettles (from which, respectively, to make linen and fine thread), yet another with a pond used for soaking withies, to make them flexible for making baskets, furniture, paddock fences, and fish traps. Separate crofts would be used for washing wool, cloth-dyeing; and tanning. In other places, the Celts put streams to use for these purposes, the activities mentioned above being strung out along their banks. One of the tutelary deities of the settlement, often Lug, represented by a wooden statue within a small grove, would preside over the scene. Small statues of this kind were many. Christian monks, once established, replaced them with wayside votive shrines dedicated to a Saint, usually St Mary, the mother of Jesus.

It seems that the many wells of Balmelllie Crofts had attracted people long before the time of the Picts. Stone Age people had settled hereabouts, as evidenced by the stone coffin, within which was an urn holding bones, unearthed in 1858 on the Turriff Haughs near the trackway mentioned, a site marked on the large scale Ordnance Survey map.

There are similar wells on the Hill of Alvah, known as St Columba's (St Colm's) Well. The same kind of activities took place here as did at Balmellie Crofts, before, during, and after, both Saints' times.

In this present day, a considerable amount of water still 'wells' up from several holes at St Colm's Well. The water authority has placed an even layer of coarse sand over them. They take up an area the size of a tennis-court which water authority has enclosed and roofed. Water from the wells constantly surfaces through the sand to make a shallow pool of even depth, from which it is piped away for the public supply.

There were similar wells at a village called Welland, near Malvern, Gloucestershire. They still exist at the cathedral town of Wells in Somerset.

Over the centuries, as water-tables throughout Britain became lower, the 'welling' holes ceased to flow. When this happened the holes were dug out to reach their vanishing waters - hence the double meaning of the word 'well' in this watery context.

In passing, four comments ought to be made:

1. the Celts were known as great cattle breeders. Annually in a religious ceremony, they immersed their cattle for the good of the animals' health, preferably in the sea; but if not, in dammed streams. St Cowan's Den would have served well for that purpose.

2. the iron-making bloomeries, mentioned earlier, would not be near Balmellie Crofts, but on higher ground at different places in different times, according to the source of charcoal and the availability of hardwoods.

3. it may be supposed the settlement itself was on the north side of the Monk's Way, away from the greater dampness of the water-bearing Balmellie Crofts.

4. the narrow Cowan's Den, with its steep sides, would not have been convenient for many activities mentioned above.

CHAPTER 9
COWAN'S OR CONGAN'S DEN, TURRIFF

It may be that St Congan came to this settlement at Balmellie Crofts with the foreknowledge that it was large enough to make preaching the Gospel very fruitful, and that passing travellers would speak of him further inland in Lathmon's territory immediately to the south; perhaps further still, amongst the people in the settlements at Bennachie.

As will be mentioned later, he would be required to live outside the settlement at Balmellie Crofts, which explains why legend has it that, when he first arrived, he established himself at the head of his eponymous watery Den. There, beside a frequented trackway that passed beside the Den, away southwards to Bennachie, he built his cell of several thatched round houses, one of which would be the church.

It would seem St Congan did not stay. Before long he and his fellow monks moved a mile westwards where they built another church on the site of a disused Pictish fort. Perhaps the local chief thought they were too near his settlement and likely to be a disturbing influence, so he made them move.

This Den is on the south side of the Balmellie road. From the lower end of Turriff graveyard is an excellent view into the Den, which is bisected by a stone wall two metres high. Beginning just short of the Balmellie road, the wall descends into the Den, passing along the eastern side of the burn, giving a false appearance of narrowness. At the edge of the haughs that border the Turriff Burn, the same wall turns westwards for 30 metres or so, and then turns northwards so as to surround the entire graveyard.

At their northern ends, these fields border a farm trackway, known as the Monks' Way. This leads eastwards for some 200 hundred metres, passing to the north of Balmellie Crofts, before turning northwards for some 500 metres, where it becomes untraceable, to continue along a very ancient lane that leads to Delgaty Castle.

This account of the history of Cowan's Den ought not to be left without mention of a strange oblong stone that a Mr F. Grant Snr uncovered some five metres below the original surface when excavating sand from the ice-age machaire above the Turriff Haughs. This stone was a hewn rock 3m by 9m by 6m of the same geological kind found just off the old road to Banff at the Delster quarry. A much smaller rock was beside it, the size and shape of a rugby football. The significance of the smaller stone remains a mystery, and no doubt will remain so as it has since disappeared. Perhaps the larger stone marked an important religious place at the settlement and that a Christian monk had it removed and buried deeply in the sand at the edge of the Haughs. On the other hand, Mr W. Davidson thinks it may have been a boundary marker from a later period. When the stone was moved it broke into three pieces. The uppermost was taken to ornament the garden of the house, 'St Congan's Den'.

In passing, it ought to be mentioned that the alluvial sand in which the rock had been buried, had strata of peaty material which suggested it was an old machaire that had been built up at the end of each succeeding ice-age when the lower River Deveron had been dammed downstream several times by ice. A deep lake formed and reformed in the lower Deveron valley and its tributaries, the water receding on each occasion allowing plants to flourish on this particular machaire, which they did for centuries, before they were overwhelmed again.

CHAPTER 10
ST CONGAN - HIS LIFE AND TIMES

St Congan (c.700), also known as Choan, Coan, Cowan, and as Comgan, is patron saint of Turriff in Aberdeenshire; and the church at Kirkton, Lochalsh, is dedicated to him. The first mention of him is in the Irish manuscripts, the Book of Leinster, the Martyrology of Gorman, the Martyrology of Oengus, the Annals of Ulster, and the Martyrology of Donegal.

The Kalendars of Scottish Saints and the Aberdeen Breviary say that St Congan was the son of Cellach Cualann (Kelly Colgan), a prince of Leinster. The Irish Martyrologies say in his youth he was trained as a soldier during which period he and his sister, St Kentigerna, became Christians. Upon succeeding his father, in his zeal for proselytizing it would seem he attacked non-Christian neighbours, as did many Christian princes in those times. In a decisive battle he was wounded in the foot, and his army conquered. The victors forced him to leave his kingdom and native country. In company with St Kentigerna, her sons Fillan, Fursey, and Ultan, and seven other clerics, he went to Lochelch (Lochalsh), in Northern Erchadia (now Wester Ross), where, it is said, they lived a severe life. After many years, St Congan died and was buried by St. Fillan in Iona. St Fillan also built a church in honour of his uncle.

No details of St Congan are mentioned in the Irish authorities. However, they record St Kentigerna as leaving Lochalsh after being 'deprived' of her son and brother', and living for many years as an anchoress on an island in Loch Lomond where she died in 734. Assuming that 'deprived' means 'died', it may be taken that Congan lived and was active as a missionary c. 700 +- 40 years.

The precise order of St Congan's movements in Scotland has not been determined yet. As a Christian prince of an Irish royal house, he would undoubtedly have come first to Iona; to the monastery founded some 150 years earlier by St. Columba in 563. The Irish monks were great navigators and as such they followed those before them in choosing Iona as the strategic centre for their missionary work into the Highlands and Islands and the North East of Scotland. In St Congan's time, probably the chief Celtic Church of Britain was at Iona, and consequently it was an important political centre.

St Congan, having the necessary education and stature to lead, appears to have been sent on missionary journeys mostly to the Western Highlands. He may not have visited every place commemorating his name; but at each of those he did, in keeping with the practice of Celtic monks, he would have had built a small beehive-shaped church of wood and thatch, a hut for the priest, and a large stone cross. Having consecrated the church, blessed the cross, the new altar, and the priest's hut, he would have moved on with his party, taking his own small altar stone with him, leaving a devoted follower in charge.

The Picts of the Highlands and Islands differed from other Celts in Scotland in that they long had contact with the Mediterranean people.

Whilst establishing his churches amongst the Picts of the Highlands and Islands, he would soon know of the migrations of some of them to the hinterland of the Moray Firth; and that every summer there were sailings between the Picts at home and the migrants. These migrations may have been the factor that brought St Congan to Turriff, because, at some time, he went on an important proselytizing mission eastwards to a Pictish prince named Lathmon, the then leader of the Pictish farmers who had been occupying land south and west of the future site of Turriff, since about 350 AD. Lathmon was a prince of the Picts living to the north of the major settlement at Bennachie.

For this purpose, St Congan would have gone first to the established monastery at Deer, an abbey-bishopric situated between the northern boundary of Lathmon's domain and the coast. A reference in the Book of Deer, written about 500 years after the event, says the monastery was founded jointly by St. Columba and St. Drostan c.575, some 120 years before St Congan's time, and that they also founded the church by the shore at New Aberdour.

Until the coming of turnpike roads, long-distance travel, wherever possible, was by boat to a convenient place along the coast from which to complete the journey inland. Two of the several landing-places that served the Pictish clans living in the hinterland as far as Bennachie and beyond, were Doun (Macduff), Gamrie (Gardenstown), and the beach at New Aberdour. The tracks from these two landing places are to Bennachie, each with a diversion to Cowan's Den, St Congan's legendary first dwelling at Turriff, mentioned earlier.

The 11th century church on the cliffs opposite Gardenstown commemorates St John the Baptist. This commemoration suggests a much earlier church was on that site. Very early churches built at landing-places and river crossings were more often than not dedicated to this saint because the 21st of June, in the middle of the travelling season, is St John the Baptist's Day. Therefore, clearly, he is the saint to invoke for help in converting listeners to Christianity. This church at the landing place at Gamrie was at the top of the easiest way up the steep coastal hills surrounding Gamrie beach, and was at the beginning of the long-distance track to Bennachie. The ruins of a later building are still to be seen.

Legend has it that Lathmon occupied Dun Lathmon, now known as the Hill of Dorlaithers ('dor', a variant of 'tor' = a steep hill), four miles south of the future site of Turriff; one of several strategic parts of his domain. The evidence, such as it is, suggests he was St Congan's contemporary. He was not the Lathmon that figures in the 'Poems of Ossian' forged by James MacPherson (c.1760).

Lathmon had the River Deveron as the western and northern boundary of his territory. That gave him control of the trackways leading to the settlements at Bennachie from Portsoy, Whitehills, Banff, Gamrie, Pennan, and New Aberdour; these coastal places being under the control of minor independent chiefs. He, most likely, had no central seat, but moved about his princedom according to need and season.

A mile and a half to the north-east of Dorlaithers is Tods Fauld (Scotch for a field that was once a fox hole, then a night cattle fold). It was an important hill-position, its lower crest at East Middletack overlooking the Doune trackway as it came from the north, and the Monks' Way, at the places where they crossed the Turriff Burn.

Wayfarers, who had landed at any of the places mentioned and were on their way to the more populated areas south of Bennachie, could be seen by Lathmon's farmer-watchmen at East Middletack when they crossed the Burn. Here they were intercepted for their news, which, if important, would be sent on speedily by a local messenger.

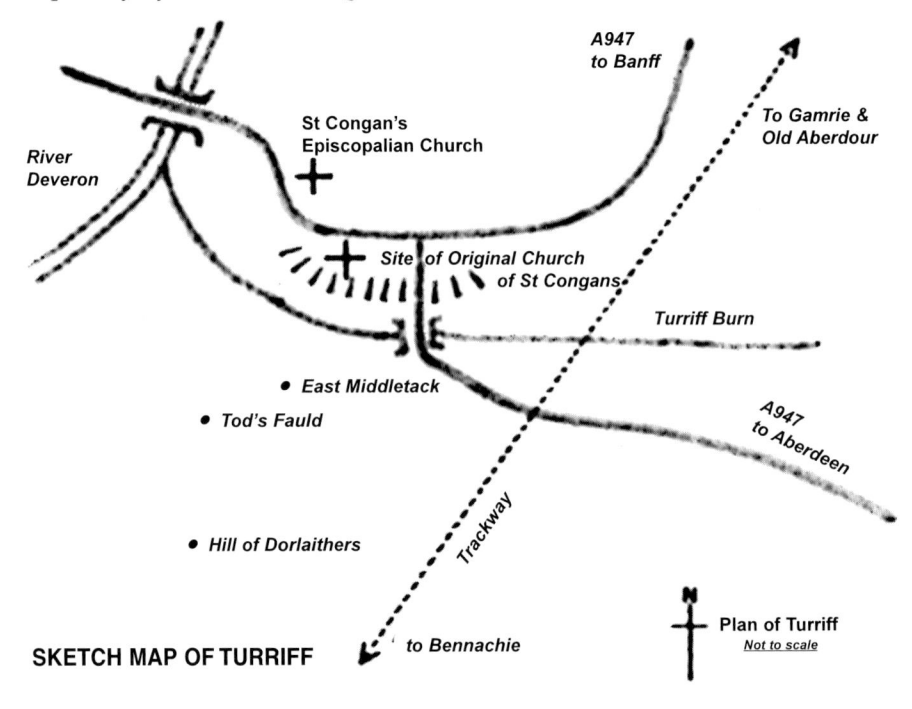

SKETCH MAP OF TURRIFF

(Sketch map showing: River Deveron, A947 to Banff, To Gamrie & Old Aberdour, St Congan's Episcopalian Church, Site of Original Church of St Congans, Turriff Burn, East Middletack, Tod's Fauld, A947 to Aberdeen, Hill of Dorlaithers, Trackway to Bennachie, Plan of Turriff — Not to scale)

Pictish princes, generally, were friendly to the Christian Church. St Congan though a monk was a member of an Irish royal family so Lathmon would have received him in fitting style. The occasion must have been a great event, talked about for years afterwards, which explains why Lathmon's name survives in legend.

Nonetheless, Lathmon would not have allowed St Congan to stay within any of his settlements because his presence might cause discord amongst the people, who were under the protection of Celtic gods and goddesses. St Congan never established his church on Lathmon's lands.

In passing, though, it is necessary to note that a certain St Carnac is said to have had a chapel dedicated to him on the Haugh of Laithers opposite the Boat of Magi. Some say it was a fifth century chapel and the church at Turriff was built to replace it. However, the New Statistical Account of Scotland says St. Carnac died in 1125 and that the ruins are 'the remains of a Druid Temple'.

Celtic missionaries, when given the opportunity, built their churches and chapels near wells so they could preach the Gospel message to the water-carriers, usually women, who came to these places frequently, or, they built at river-crossings where wayfarers might be greeted for the same purpose. St Congan would have done similarly. His mission to these parts is dealt with in detail later.

When it came to a permanent place for his church, St Congan chose a prominent ridge at the edge of the Turriff Burn on what was once a Pictish fort. This position had the added advantage that his church building could be seen clearly by the people at Lathmon's outpost at East Middletack.

This Pictish fort was not occupied. Had it been, Lathmon would not have given it up. It had been abandoned years earlier because of a much reduced population. Very recent research suggests world-wide sunless days and bad harvests, caused by clouds of minute dust particles high in the atmosphere from a massive eruption of Krakatoa in 535/6, led to many deaths everywhere by famine. Even more deaths occurred from the Yellow Plague, the 'Pesta Flava', as noted by the monks. Not one of the bubonic variety such as the Black Death of the Middle Ages, it arrived in Britain from Europe in 547, reaching Scotland in 551/2. It is said it was preceded by "the appearance of a vaporous column sweeping along the ground, discharging heavy rain in its wake". All within its path sickened to death, including animals.

Some 150 years later, in St Congan's time, the population may not have recovered its numbers sufficiently to re-occupy this isolated fort immediately outside the perimeter of the Princedom, and for this reason may not have been needed as a fort.

The site was ideal, it having a fertile dell near at hand that the monks might cultivate. The Old Rectory manse stands at its edge. The dell is the place about which Turriff began and is now full of buildings. Until recently, a market garden had long been a part of it, which suggests a long period of cultivation.

St Congan consecrated his church and then, as was the practice, left it in charge of another monk, returning to Lochalsh where eventually he died. Fillan, his nephew, took his body to Iona for burial. That he did so, speaks of Congan's great importance in the Celtic church.

Some infer there was monastery at Turriff because in 1131 the Book of Deer mentions a monk, Donongart of Turriff, (fer-léighinn = vir-legendi = a man of learning), witnessing a grant to Deer. St Congan's church was rebuilt at about the same time by King Malcolm Canmore III (s.1057. d.1137) so it would seem there was much religious activity at Turriff then. However Celtic humorous exaggeration in conversation may have dignified a church and a few small dwellings into a monastery. A dearth of archaeological and written evidence makes it impossible to say there was ever more than a church at Turriff or Cowan's Den.

Significantly, an ancient path still known as 'The Wynd' ran through the centre of this dell. Today it begins in the Main Street, but, in time gone by it was a minor path from Congan's Den to the dwellings in the dell and St Congan's Church.

The word 'wynd' has implications. It suggests a path criss-crossing the little burn, 'winding' between large circular paddocks each surrounding a hut. Surviving examples of a wynd of this kind can be seen at Sedbergh in Cumbria. As others do, over time the wynd at Turriff became straightened. The little burn flowed across Castle Street, where it was a ford, and down what is now Woolmill Road, to the Turriff Haughs. Now it flows underground through a storm water culvert. Its route can be traced by following the manhole covers set at intervals down the Woollmill Road. A marshy hollow beside an ancient bank set at an angle at the bottom of the hill, marks the place where its waters once joined the Turriff Burn.

Over the centuries the water table has become lower and the Turriff Burn, itself, is no longer the size it was. Its flow has been further reduced because of agricultural improvements to land upstream during the 19th Century when bogs and fields were drained. Many pipes for this purpose were made at the Whitehills brickworks near the old dock hewn out of rock.

In Castle Street, immediately uphill from the beginning of Woollmill Road, fastened to the wall of brown stone cottages, there is a street-nameplate bearing the words 'Putachie Path'.

'Putachie' is Celtic for 'cattle-fold (much corrupted from 'acha' = a burn + 'chuit' = fold). This fold, most likely, was in Woollmill Road at a steep-sided place, under the Pictish fort. This may have been the town 'shambles', or butchery. It is said that, in Scotland, there are only three other places with the name 'Putachie'. The ford must have had a particularly steep approach because the cottages mentioned are isolated high above Castle Street. In addition, the narrow path in front of the cottages comes to a dead end, also suggesting that below this place, Castle Street is now lower than it was at its original level.

St Congan was a Culdee, ('Ceile-de' = servant of God), as the monks of the Celtic Church were known from the 8th century onwards. The word 'Saint', in this Celtic connection, means 'holy man'. A corruption, 'cully', meaning friend and colleague, was in current usage in the English language until the 18th century.

Regardless of stature, Culdee monks would have similar personal appearances. They would be thin because of their rule to keep their bodies 'under control' by privation and fasting. The hair shirt was often worn. The Culdees often immersed themselves in cold water to the neck; a regular happening at wells and rivers sacred to the Celts, especially at places where the local druids made votive offerings to Celtic deities. This deliberate polluting of the waters was intended to defile the god or goddess of the place and show how powerless it was against the insults of Christianity.

Most noticeable about St Congan would be his long face, an impression created by a short beard and curved bald pate, which, taken overall, had a distinct resemblance to an adze, a tool once commonly used to work timber. This effect was caused because the Celtic tonsure required the front of the head to be shaven, over the top, from ear to ear, earning the wearer the nick-name, 'Adze-Head'. The Roman tonsure, on the other hand, required merely the crown of the head to be shaved. The purpose of a tonsure was so that Christianized soldiers could easily recognise a man outside the combat and not put him to the sword.

Ancient fashion is sometimes preserved in strange ways by custom. In a leaflet about his Church, dated 1983, the Reverend Dr Lamont, minister of Strath, Trumpan, in Skye says that, in Victorian times and earlier, many ministers of the churches in Skye sporting side-whiskers, scrupulously shaved the upper lip. The Reverend Lamont suggests this practice was a harking back to the tradition of the Culdee tonsure.

Like most early Celtic monks, St Congan would be dressed in a white tunic with a cowl. He would have a mantle (amphibalus/chasuble), of sheepskin, goatskin, or fawnskin, thrown over the shoulder in cold weather. There would be a wallet at his side containing a beautifully-inscribed Psalter. He would have had a vestment and a breastplate to wear at services, both decorated. He would carry a crozier and have a liturgical fan called a flabellum or rhipidion. This was a short staff with a wide fan-like head formed of jewelled and decorated feathery fronds of flexible metal representing a peacock's tail. The metal 'feathers' were for fidelity. They bowed constantly in adoration, as is said the winged seraphim did before the Christ-child. The jewels represented eyes for vigilance. The peacock itself, of course, symbolized immortality. The Celtic church traced its beginnings from the hermit-monks who lived in the wildernesses of Egypt and similar places, where, during the liturgy, they each used the fan to protect their altars and offerings from flies, dust, and the forces of evil. Tradition made it a part of every saint's equipment, which is how it came from Egypt to Scotland.

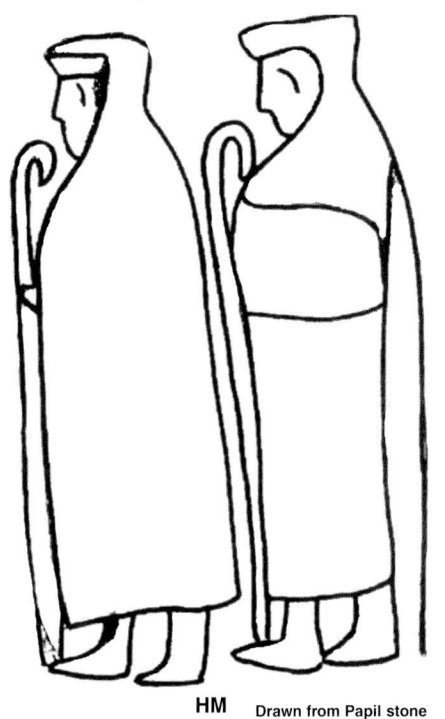

HM   Drawn from Papil stone

St Congan also took with him, as did every Celtic saint on his travels, a round, portable altar-stone which his followers would carry. Another in his party would bear his large silver bell. Every Celtic saint had one. Usually it was decorated and inscribed. In the sparsely populated lands of Celtic Britain the ordinary traveller used an iron clapper bell so those in wooded areas nearby were aware of his presence and would know he was not lurking as a thief.

The first intimation the inhabitants of a Pictish settlement would have of the approach of a Culdee saint would be a silvery, bewitching, ethereal sound coming from an unseen source at a distance. It would have a profound effect upon those who had never heard anything like it. The saint, when he came amongst them, would have had no difficulty in persuading an already intensely superstitious people that benign spirits called angels of Christ were nearby. Whether they would abandon their own gods and goddesses for them was a different matter.

The Celtic church conducted missionary work from a great monastery, such as Deer Abbey. Its buildings usually were a cluster of 'beehive' huts, a church of wood and stone, a well nearby, a refectory, a hospital, a cemetery, and at the centre, a great stone cross; all within an encircling wall, which in Ireland, is called a rath. The abbot was the real leader and the bishop the senior missionary. There was no territorial limit of jurisdiction for a monastery; for instance, it was not until the 12th century that the Roman Church divided Ireland into dioceses.

Contention arose between the Roman and Celtic churches; the given causes were they differed as to the dates for Easter, the shape of the tonsure, and the method of baptism. The Celtic church gave complete immersion in water and preferred adult candidates; the Roman church sprinkled water, preferably upon children. However, some think that the fundamental reason for the conflict was that, unlike the Celtic church, the Roman church was mercenary, as Luther claimed later.

In Britain, this dispute between the churches came to a head in 664, at the Council of Whitby. The Celtic Church lost the debate and had to submit to Roman ways, which, in time, were imposed everywhere. The Celtic church disappeared from Western Europe. It is worth noting that Wilfred, leader of the Roman faction at Whitby, died leaving a massive fortune, even though the church of which he was a member did not allow its priests personal money.

By 715, in Congan's time, Nectan, King of the Picts, had imposed the Roman Easter throughout Scotland. Although he expelled the Church of Iona in 717 for refusing to conform, Nectan tolerated its Culdees in the north because their organisation was fluid, they were allowed personal money and could finance themselves, which cost him nothing, and because there were not yet enough priests of the Roman church to replace them.

It was often Celtic practice for the succeeding monk to be known by the name of the founding father. Some of the first missionaries found it expedient to take the name of the Celtic deity that Christianity was supplanting: as happened when Bridget, a powerful Celtic goddess, was canonized and became St Bridget; and, in Cornwall, Yew (a tree) became St Yew. This seemed to have been the case at Turriff because the church was not rededicated to another saint, as many were, which caused certain anomalies to arise in connection with the date of 'Cowan's (Congan's) Fair, as explained below.

Every Saint had his commemoration day, often a holiday in the secular sense. The Irish Martyrologies give August the 2nd for St Congan's holy day, long celebrated at Turriff as 'Cowan's Fair', that is until recently. However, the later Aberdeen Breviary says he is commemorated on October 13th.

The reason for the differing days goes back to when the Roman Church first began rededicating the churches in Scotland it had taken over from the Culdees with the names of saints on the Vatican's approved list, a continuing process. However, no saint on this list replaced St Congan, perhaps local feeling in opposition was too strong.

In such cases where the first Roman priest finds he is obliged to retain the Culdee saint's name, he usually insisted upon a change to mark his own coming to the church. This is achieved by moving the Culdee saint's day to the one on which he has been inducted; in the case at Turriff, October the 13th.

In this connection, The New Statistical Account of Scotland also records 'St Cowan's Fair' as being on the 2nd of August, confirming the record in the Irish Martyrologies. It also says it was renamed St Peter's Fair in 1511. This was one of the cases in which the Roman Church intended to obliterate the memory, the memory of Celtic Saints. However the people clung to tradition and held 'Cowan's fair' on the 2nd of August. From the same entry in the New Statistical Account one notes that the Roman church had succeeded in substituting a Saint's name for Cowan from its approved list, but only for the Fair.

Later 'Lammas Fair', which was held on the last Tuesday in July, was merged with St Peter's (Cowan's) Fair. When farming thrived, the joint fair became known as the Turriff Show.

Perhaps, one day the Turriff Show will revert to its ancient name, 'Cowan's Fair', to mark its antiquity.

From on high on the Sandstone War Memorial at the entrance to the graveyard beside his Den, a statue of St Congan has been placed so it faces across the Turriff Haughs, where the Show is held, towards Lathmon's lands beyond.

CHAPTER 11
A SOCIAL SCOURGE OF ANCIENT TIMES

Before leaving St Congan and his times, mention should be made of the ways in which people in Britain dealt with cases of extreme madness. These, when they occurred, were the trials beyond endurance. The weak-minded were manageable, but there were no people free of work to keep a full-time watch on fire-raisers, and the violent psychopath.

A clue as to what was done to rid a village of such a dangerously mad person lies in the legend of the death of Merlin, the magician associated with King Arthur and the Knights of the Round Table. In Scotland he was known also as Lailoken, an extraordinary seer of the Picts.

As a Druid, he was a non-combatant, at the battle of Arfdydd (573) that took place nine miles north of Carlisle. He became mad after the battle having witnessed what he would never have believed possible - Christianized Celts slaughtering Celts who were not; contrary to the humane rules of engagement in battle by which they had fought for centuries. Not striking a man when he is down, and the term, 'fair play' are both Celtic codes of behaviour in battle.

It should be mentioned in passing, that in these times Christian Celts were enthusiastic about making war, which they often did recklessly, on those who had not been converted to the faith. The oldest Scottish poem, the Goddoddin, records how a Scottish king at Edinburgh feasted and spiritually prepared three hundred men for a year and then sent them to attack the non-Christian Yorkshire men, who, outnumbering them 33 to 1, defeated them at Catterick (590).

During the period of madness he suffered after the battle, Merlin predicted his own death on three separate occasions. On the first he said he would die by a blow, on the second by a stab, and on the third by drowning. In the event, he was attacked on the banks of the Tweed by three shepherds, one of whom struck him on the head. He fell into the river and was pierced by a fish-stake as he did so; simultaneously dieing from the killing blow, the mortal wound from the fish-stake, and drowning. Merlin was buried sy Powsail Water, near Drumelzier on the Scottish Borders.

This particular legend of an insane man being done to death in three ways relates to the many well-preserved human bodies, found recently in ancient bogs, most of the victims having been killed in three ways, usually, a blow on the head, a stab, and strangulation, which was a substitute for drowning.

Murder by three assailants, tacitly approved over many generations, was the traditional way of disposing of the dangerous insane; the responsibility in each case being shared between the three men participating. Shakespeare implied all of this when he wrote of Julius Caesar's saying at his end, "et tu Bruti", to Brutus, encouraging him to be the third assassin.

Although disposing a body in a bog ensures no evidence, in every case there would have to be a conspiracy for the deed to be done secretly; a secret reinforced by crediting fairies and spirits with abductions of persons that had mysteriously disappeared. Nearer the time of the coming of Christianity, perhaps a simultaneous murder of one person by three fellow villagers became too difficult, too elaborate, for it to be arranged. Certainly, this practice ceased, and instead the insane were openly drowned in public without ceremony.

Drowning the insane who were dangerous, continued, as required, for centuries. The fortified house, Eden Castle in Banffshire, now a ruin, has a legend, dating to the 11th century, about a laird who deliberately drowned, in the Deveron, an insane lad who had become a dangerous nuisance.

The legend of this drowning in the Deveron is thought to be from a time earlier than the 11th century because there came yet another, a third, change of practice, a Christian innovation, current everywhere in St Congan's time.

In Christian times, instead of being drowned, the insane were put into shallow pools, called bowsening pools. Standing waist high in the water, they were required to pick up stones, as best they could, from the bottom and put them on the bank. They were not big stones. The purpose was to make sure those undertaking the cure were thoroughly soaked. After a while, they were brought out and put into a building, usually the church which was nearby, and there they were left overnight, wet through. If they were thought sane in the morning, a cure had taken place; if not, the process was repeated until it had been effected, or pneumonia killed them. This cure was speedier if done in winter.

One such pool, no longer there, is recorded as being at St Fillans, beside Loch Earn, Perthshire, where St Fillan, nephew of Congan established a church. There is another near the church at Alternun, once a remote hamlet on Bodmin Moor Cornwall. This pool was renovated in the 1970's and is now a tourist attraction.

Almost every village had its bowsening pool. Each served the same purpose - the cure of the insane that were a danger to others. With so many isolated communities, inbreeding, and its consequences, feeble-mindedness and insanity, were facts of life that had to be addressed using the means available at the time.

This treatment of the insane ceased late in the Middle Ages. Even then there was an echo from the past. As late as the 18th century, eccentrics, slightly muddled women, especially scolds, were put in ducking stools and 'ducked' for a short time in the village bowening pool - the ducking pond - not so as to drown, but in the hope that this 'water' treatment would bring about their better behaviour if not a cure.

The practice died out, but many ponds survived. Before 1900 there was hardly a village in England that did not have its duck pond or its idiot.

CHAPTER 12
RIVER DEVERON AND THE TOWN OF BANFF

This expanded second edition of 'The Life and Times of St Congan' would not be complete without an explanation of how the River Deveron came by its name.

The 1826 Ordnance survey, the oldest for Banffshire, names the river as the 'Dovern'. This corruption of the Old Gaelic 'dovre' + 'an', meaning 'water of'' begs the question, 'The water of what or whose?' That great Gaelic scholar W.J. Watson provides clues in his 'History of the Celtic Place-Names of Scotland', that suggest an answer.

Starting from the beginning, the first regular visitors to these shores, as has been said, were pre-Christian Irish Celts who came long before the Picts arrived. Some brought their gods and goddesses and stayed. They founded settlements and gave them Irish names. W.J. Watson, comments upon this and says that the whole of Pictland once stood a chance of being called 'Eire', and the district east of Breadalbane did have that name. He also remarks that Tolachherene, an old Irish-Celtic name meaning 'Hill of Éire', appears to have been near the River Deveron. This, most likely, was none other than the Hill of Alvah.

Some of these visiting Irish Celts settled on high ground on a Stone Age site, ancient in their time, above the mouth of the river known later as the Deveron, which, at that time, had no name.

The River Deveron at that time, and until recently, had a narrow entrance close to the Banff side. In even earlier times it had an immense grass-covered machaire that was attached to the Macduff shore. It seems that, at the end of one of the ice-ages, ice dams broke upstream, the resulting flood waters depositing sediment when the waters reached the open sea. Later lowering sea-levels exposed these sandy deposits as a raised level called a machaire. The last vestige of this particular one is near the Deveron Bridge on the Macduff side. It is a small raised level, some fifteen feet above high water, upon which cars are parked occasionally. Over the ages, storms eroded the Deveron machaire into a sand bar, there until after 1826 according to the Ordnance Survey, after which it was swept away and the estuary's shape radically changed. The machaire at Calgary on the Isle of Mull is being similarly eroded.

While the machaire was there, the entrance to the Deveron was not obvious. However, immediately to seaward of the present Banff harbour, on a raised beach, long since eroded to its underlying bare rock, was a prominence that served these people of ancient times as a convenient marker. This they called Meavie Point, a Celtic word meaning 'sea or way mark'. Weathered over thousands of years into a flat half-tide rock, it still has its name on the OS maps. Similarly, fishermen at Kilkennie in Fife used the steeple of their church as a leading mark, calling it 'Meavie'; the church being built on an earlier, pre-Christian site used for the same purpose.

These Irish immigrants called their settlement Banbha, which was reasonable and consistent, because her name was the first by which Ireland was known. According to a lost manuscript, Amergin, son of Miled, a judge and poet, met Banbha, a manifestation of a triple goddess known as Sovereignty, when he and his people were coming to Ireland. He promised to name the land after each goddess, and called it firstly, 'the island of Banbha of the women'.

Sovereignty's names are; Éire, meaning 'beautiful', or, 'quickening', as in 'springing into life'; Fodhla, 'fodder', meaning food; and Banbha, meaning 'mystery'. Banbha had to do with agricultural mysteries that, in previous times, were matters for women. The maiden Éire was associated with the green corn, the nymph Fodhla with the ripe ear of grain, and Banbha was associated with the harvest.

The idea of shape-shifting has its origins in the mystery of the life cycle of a grain of barley. It was a Celtic custom, at the very moment when the last sheaf was gathered, to make a corn-dolly secretly and present it ceremonially to the chief harvesters. In the presence of all, it would be buried, again with ceremony, as Banbha, the third aspect of the triple-goddess Sovereignty. In yet another ceremony in early Spring, this same buried corn-dolly would be uncovered and, of course, it was found to be sprouting; transformed by unexplained magic into Éire, Sovereignty's first aspect.

In her aspect as a beautiful crone, Banbha became associated with swine. Pigs root up the soil in their search for delicacies such as truffles. Because of this activity they were believed to know about the Underworld, and hence, death. The Celts took note, and in most parts of Europe they sacrificed a pig as part of a burial rite. This custom continued into Roman times. Cicero, a contemporary of Julius Cæsar, writes; "Places of burial do not really become graves until the proper rites are performed and the pig is slain." (Cicero, Laws; XXII, Loeb 56-57, footnote). An Irish myth says that the heroes Brian, Iuchar, and Incharba, took this triple-goddess to wife, each taking her in one of her forms. Some think these marriages refer to the time when men usurped women's place on the land.

This powerful triple-goddess was present all over Europe under different names. As Kore, Demeter and Hecate, she was venerated in ancient Greece in benign ceremonies, recorded as having taken place biennially at Eleusis near Athens, for over two thousand years.

St Adamnan, known also as St Adomnan, not a contemporary of St Congan, toured north east of Scotland some 40 years before the latter arrived. He described the Grampian and wrote about the descendants of the pre-Christian Irish living there. He noted that, in the Grampian, a name with the suffix 'die' ('dee') meant the Picts there considered it denoted a goddess-place or goddess-river. He cites a particularly small burn named Boyndie as example, and says on its bank is a settlement called Inverboyndie.

This is an extraordinary statement: the burn is unworthy of deification, it being but a trickle of water nowhere near the size and importance of the vastly larger river now known as the Deveron, a little way to the east.

St Adamnan never mentions this large river in his writings, although he must have sailed past its estuary and stayed at the settlement on the bank of its estuary more than once on his way to and from the west bank of the Cromarty Firth and the beach at Aberlour Bay, the landing place for the Monastery at Deer. This omission is very strange if only because the historian and cartographist, Ptolemy, who lived 500 years earlier at Alexandria in Egypt, (c.140 AD), had already noted on his map of the world a major river here, which he named the 'Buvinda'. Some scholars accept 'Buvinda' as a variant of buandea, the collective name of the Irish river goddesses, of which Boyndie was one, as has been said. It is said there is confusion about whether it was the River Spey Ptolemy favoured with the name "Buvinda' or the River Deveron, but the proximity of Inverboyndie indicates he meant the latter, as is explained below.

From St Adamnan's account and these circumstances, it would seem that an unknown monk decided that the 'lasting goddess' Boyndie had to be shown as not 'lasting' at all. Publicly denigrating Celtic gods and goddesses was a standard practice of the Christian Church. In this instance there was no better way of demonstrating the power of Christ than peremptorily transferring the name of the goddess, and that of her eponymous settlement, to an insignificant burn nearby in the parish of St Brandon.

Culdee monks had strong personalities and great persuasive powers: the changes were made. The settlement on the Deveron was no longer to be known as Inverboyndie but as Banff. The name 'Boyndie' was banned. Thereafter, when mentioning the river, the people, dutifully uttered the first two syllables 'dovre an' (= 'water of'), which, over time, corrupted into 'Dovern', and then into 'Deveron'.

In passing it should be mentioned that more small burns hereabouts are also called Boyndie; named so later, after the Dovre an Boyndie became the Deveron as part of the continuing process of demeaning of the goddess.

She is remembered in Brittany under just the one Celtic name, Gwénolé = Gwen o' Lait (milk). For expediency's sake, she was Christianized and the monk founding the monastery assumed her name, he being known as St Gwénolé. A wooden statue of her as a goddess with three breasts, reminders of her triple aspect, is to be seen in the museum at the Benedictine monastery of Landévennec, not far from the city of Brest. The monastery building, founded in 818, destroyed by Napoleon, was rebuilt in the 1950's.

There is another Irish connection with Greece and Spain. A legend says that one of the earliest people to emigrate to Ireland were the Firbolg (people of the bags) who, as slaves in Greece, were engaged there in moving earth; that is, until they made ships of their bags, as the legend has it, and fled in them to Ireland via Spain. Some say the language of the Basques of northern Spain has affinities with Erse, the Gaelic of the Irish. The geographer, Strabo, (c.63BC - 24AD) writes that the Romans found the Basques, more than most, an unruly and aggressive people; leading one to reflect on the recent histories of the Irish and the Basque peoples. Put side by side with Strabo's comments, the unruliness of certain people in northern Ireland and in northern Spain, during the latter half of the 20th century begs interesting questions.

The Irish Celts, having chosen the name of the goddess Banbha for their settlement, decided upon the name of a particular group of 'lasting and sacred' Irish Celtic goddesses known as the Buandea for the name of the river that flowed close by into the Moray Firth, the 'Dovre an Boyndie', the 'Water of the Lasting and Sacred Goddesses'.

Times and customs change. Some hundreds of years later the Picts occupied the settlement and added 'inver' to 'boyndie', so the place was known as both Banff and Inverboyndie. This change to two names was in keeping with the then common practice of every person and every abode having two names, one that was true and secretive, and another for daily use to deceive eaves-dropping evil spirits and deflect their evil attentions. The practice survived in Britain until very recently in that, outside the family, no one was ever addressed by a first name except by definite invitation. As is well known this practice survives in the French language by the use of 'tu' and 'vous'.

Long after the Irish pre-Christian Celts came to the North East of Scotland, Irish monks, following the Picts, came here by way of Iona. The famous Irish saint, St Brandon, or Brendan the Voyager, was one of the first to come. He became the patron saint of Boyndie Parish where he is said to have preached at a stone-age site called the 'Brannan Stones'. St Brendan habitually sailed the trade routes, presumably in his leather-hulled curach. It is said he visited Wales and Cornwall, and also France which he did in the company of St Malo.

Another early Christian visitor was St Adamnan (c.660): who, it is said, succeeded St Columba as Abbot at Iona.

Reading between the lines, it would seem St Adamnan himself had made the changes. Forbidding the use of a name was common practice in both Celtic and Roman Churches in Europe and Britain. The Celtic Church forbade Celtic heathen names. In Germany, the name of the city of Essen ('eas' = 'water' + 'an' = 'of') is a case where a name is missing. In Britain, the Roman church, authorised by the Synod of Whitby (664) to be the only Christian authority, used that method of forbidding the use of a name, more than any other, to destroy the Celtic Church, its monks, and the people's memory of them.

There are examples of this practice. One such occurred in Liskeard, a town in Celtic Cornwall. Today it has a Lux Place. 'Lux' on its own means 'place', being a Celtic corruption of 'Loc' [Latin 'locus' = 'place of (someone)']. The name of the 'someone' is that of the Celtic monk, St Silin. Lux Place was once Locsilin (St Silin's Place) until a priest of the Roman Church forbade the name 'Silin' to be uttered. Thereafter, the people referred to it as 'Lux'. In their time, the Saxons added the word 'Place' which is superfluous. Some fifteen miles further west of Liskeard the tiny parish of Luxulyan (Loc-Silin) escaped the same treatment; probably because at that time it was remote and in strongly-held Viking territory.

These same Vikings, sometimes Christians and sometimes not, were defeated by the Saxon king, Athelstan (895 - 940), in three pitched battles. He fought them to prevent their uniting and forming a Princedom in Cornwall and thus legalizing their piracies. It should be mentioned in passing that the defeated Vikings left for Brittany where they were defeated again with the help of troops sent by Athelstan. Leaving Brittany they settled in Normandy with the permission of the French king and became the Normans of history.

To return to the history of the eradication of the memory of Celtic saints; beginning in the 14th Century, throughout the centuries the Roman Church rededicated as many churches of Culdee origin as it could giving each the name of a saint appearing on its approved list, such as Andrew, George, Martin, and Jerome. Referring to Cornwall again for example, in 1328, the Parish church at Liskeard, believed to have been dedicated to St Silin, was rededicated to St Martin and its Saint's Day changed accordingly.

As part of the programme of romanizing, St George and St Andrew became the patron saints of England and Scotland respectively; the latter being preferred to those great saints of Scotland, St Ninian and St Columba. The Saint's Day at St Congan's Church, Turriff was moved to another day for a similar reason, though there in no record of a rededication.

CHAPTER 13
ST CONGAN'S DEN - THE MODERN DWELLING

(This account is published as an addendum by kind permission of Mr and Mrs W. Davidson).

The Den was considered a place of natural beauty; so much so, that in 1918 a Dr Robert and Mrs Mary Keith, captivated by its charm, purchased the only dwelling there at the time, and set about modernizing it. Plans and papers are extant and are in the possession of Mr and Mrs W. Davidson, the present owners who so kindly made them available. They include the architect's plan of the house and its interior, before the proposed alterations, together with a coloured drawing of the front elevation.

The drawings show a typical Scottish long house dating from the 1700's, or earlier. It was built with its long axis parallel to the lie of the Den. The interior was shown to consist of a large kitchen with a boxed-in bed-space opposite the fireplace. A short passage on the east side of the bed-space led to a dairy. Another on the west side led to a room presumably used as a parlour. A narrow flight of stairs rose to a roof space lit by two skylights. Below the same roof were a barn, a byre, and a poultry house, in that order, each separated by an interior wall.

This type of house, incorporating barn and byre, typical of a sheiling, was common in country districts in Scotland until the turn of the 19th century. It was the successor of the Celtic long house in use before and after St Congan's time, in which the occupants slept above the cattle in their byres, for warmth.

The property came with twelve acres of land that bordered the lower part of the Collie Stripe (Celtic, 'collie' = hill + 'stripe' = stream) and the Turriff Haughs. Mrs Keith relinquished these acres as Cowan's Den. In due course they became the site of an housing estate with a road bearing that name and two more called St Congan's Den, and St Congan's Circle.

Workmen completely gutted the interior of the long house and rebuilt it to a new plan which incorporated the barn, byre, and poultry house into additional living spaces. In addition, the roof was raised to make a proper upper floor with bedrooms and a bathroom.

The most modern kitchen range of the time was installed which would provide a constant and ample supply of hot water in the kitchen and for a bath upstairs to which it was piped. A contemporary illustration of the kitchen range is amongst the papers. A flushing lavatory was installed upstairs, in place of the traditional; two-seater, earth-closet that would be at the end of the garden.

For all these domestic arrangements, novelties for a small house at the time, Mrs Keith required a constant supply of fresh water. This she provided by commissioning an hydraulic ram, that is, an automatic pump - the nearest thing to perpetual motion - to be placed in the burn in the Den, the water from there to be piped uphill to the kitchen range, and to the bath and toilet upstairs.

The quotation to supply, dated 1918, which is extant, undertook to install a ram that would deliver 100 gallons a day to the house through an half inch pipe to a height of 46 feet, a cost of £7 pounds and 16 shillings.

Mrs Keith, now having more water than she needed, had the perpetual overflow piped off to a cistern that one of her sons constructed in shuttered concrete further down the Den. A door in the graveyard wall was made through which members of the general public could pass to draw water from it.

In very recent times the flow of water within the Den had been led through a man-made pond at the site of the cistern. The water from this pond fed a sluice for washing sand, a major operation that has now ceased. Drainage work in 2004 removed the very ancient marsh at the lower end of the Den.

In addition, sand and gravel extraction from the ancient machaire has much altered the appearance of the land immediately to the east of the dwelling at St Cowan's Den which is beside the ancient trackway that led across the Turriff Haughs. Heights everywhere have been lowered by these operations, excepting those of the graveyard, a place from which one may overlook the surrounding land and obtain an idea of previous levels. In short, the lie of the land adjacent to the Den nowhere resembles that in St Congan's time.

Mrs Keith, it is said, firmly believed her house was on the site of St Congan's Abbey. It would seem that this was a supposition of her own that she put about.

It was she who changed the name of the house from Cowan's to St Congan's Den. During the fifty odd years or so she lived under its roof as a widow, she created a beautiful garden in the Den, which she opened to the public once a year at an admission charge of sixpence each, the proceeds to be given to the Red Cross.

Mrs Keith, and the successive residents in her house, were and are very positive about the benign atmosphere of the Den. Others say similarly when viewing the Den from the lower graveyard, the best overall vantage place.

By 1981, there had been many nearby changes. The fields round about Balmellie Road nearer Turriff had been developed into housing estates. The twelve acres known as Cowan's Den had no less than three separate commercial sandpits. Extraction of sand from these pits continued until the year 2000, by which time the land had been lowered and levelled, in some places by as much as 10 metres.

Since Mrs Keith's time the dwelling 'St Cowan's Den' has been extended and modernized a second and a third time. During the most recent alterations, the present owners say that further to the south they came across unbelievably hard stones mixed with cinders, which they supposed had been dumped there from old brickworks that once existed nearby. Immediately to the east of the house they came across the remains of a circle twenty feet in diameter, made of stone not unlike cobbles; possibly the remains of a Celtic roundhouse; the foundations, perhaps, of one of St Congan's dwellings.

ABRIDGED BIBLIOGRAPHY

Aberdeen Breviary, ed William Bishop of Aberdeen, 1509,
        Bannatyre Club and Spalding Club.
Acta Sanctorum, The Bollandists, [Vol VI pp. 223-6, (64 vols). Antwerp 1794].
The Age of the Picts, by W.A Cummins, Alan Sutton, Ltd. 1995.
The Ancient Explorers by Cary & Warmington, British Library.
Ancient Greek France, by A.Trevor Hodge.
The Report of the Argyle Royal Commission.
Arthur and the Britons in Wales and Scotland, W.F. Skene,
        Llanerch Enterprises, Lampeter, Dyfed, SA48 8PJ. 1998.
'Bloomeries', Transactions of the Banffshire Field Club 1902.
The Book of Deer, reproduced on website www.bookofdeer.co.uk.
The Book of Leinster, facsimile of J. O'Longan's copy, Royal Irish Academy.
Carthage by B. H. Warmington. British Library
Celtic Journeys - Scotland and the North of England 1985, Shirley T. Hutchinson.
Celtic Place-Names in Aberdeenshire, Aberdeen Daily Journal, J. Milne. 1912.
Celtic Scotland by W. F. Skene.
The Gallic War, the Civil Wars by Julius Cæsar, (two vols.) Loeb Classical Library.
Daily Life in Carthage at the time of Hannibal, Gilbert & Colette Charles-Picard,
        George Allen & Unwin 1958.
The 'Dualchas' Collection, Skye and Lochalsh Museums' Service.
The Greek Myths, Robert Graves, Penguin Books 1955.
Historic Oddities and Strange Events, 1889, S. Baring-Gould.
Historical Monuments (Scotland) Commission.
The History of the Celtic Place Names of Scotland,
        W.J.Watson, Irish Academic Press, Dublin, 1986. (Banbh, Inverboyndie).
Irish Lives of the Saints of Ireland, ed C. Plummer.
In Search of the Picts, C. Sutherland.
Kalendars of Scottish Saints, ed A. P. Forbes, pp. 310-31, 1872.
Krakatoa Global Catastrophe ITV Channel 4. (25.5.2000).
The Legend of Eden Castle, 'Ruined Castles' by James Spence , 1872,
        Copy in Banff Library.
The Leopard Magazine February 1994, 'Turriff', Stewart Michell.
Libraire Hachette, Royal National Library, Brussels 1958.
Lives of the Saints, Vol IV, p. 104, Butler,
        revised by H. Thurston and D. Attwater, 1953-4.
'St. Martin's Parish Church Guide', Liskeard, Cornwall, William Paynter.
Martyrology of Donegal, ed H. Tod, Irish Archaeological Society.
Martyrology of Gorman, ed Whitley Stokes, Henry Bradshaw Society.
Martyrology of Oengus the Culdee, ed Witley Stokes.

The Millbrook Ship-Model, H. Garner,
    Devon & Cornwall Notes and Queries, volume XXXVIII. Part V, 1999.
The New Statistical Account of Scotland.
The Oxford Dictionary of Saints.
Rome in Africa, Susan Raven, Routledge, 1993.
The Saints of Cornwall, Canon G. Doble, Truro Cathedral.
The Sea Roads of the Saints, J. Marsden, 1995, Floris Books.
Scottish Land Names by Sir Herbert Maxwell , Blackwood London 1894.
Secrets of the Dead, ITV Channel 4 (18.5.2000).
Tin in Antiquity by R D Penhalligan, 1986.
Pytheas Von Massilia, Collegit, Hans Joachim Mette, Walter de Gruyter & Co.
    Berlin, 1952.